THE
GUILDFORD
GUY RIOTS

Being an Exact Description of the terrible
Disturbances in the County Town of Surrey

BY GAVIN MORGAN

WITH ILLUSTRATIONS

GUILDFORD: 1992

ACKNOWLEDGEMENTS

This book is dedicated to my parents, my sisters and to the memory of my grandparents. I would like to thank Matthew Alexander and Eric Hunter of Guildford Museum and Richard Sharp of the Metropolitan Police Historical Museum. I am also grateful to Sally Fentiman, John Chase, Richard Stroud, Margaret Meyer and Ian Ridley for helping to produce the book. Finally, I would especially like to thank John Janaway for his generous advice throughout the production process.

FIRST PUBLISHED 1992

Copyright © Gavin Morgan 1992

NORTHSIDE BOOKS
19 Northside
Clapham Common
London SW4 ORQ

ISBN 0 9520205 0 5

Printed and bound in England by
Staples Printers Rochester Ltd

CONTENTS

GUILDFORD IN 1870

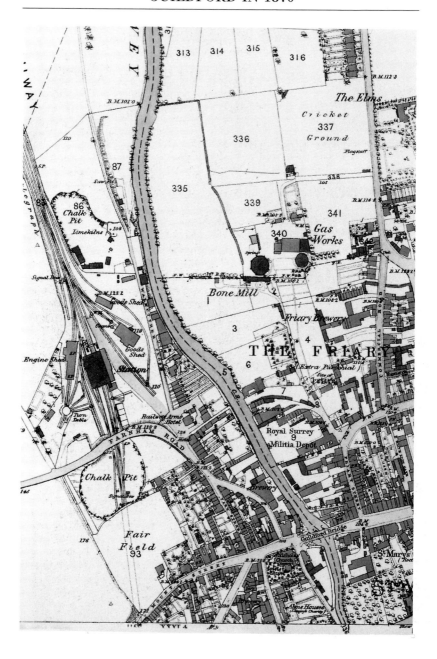

Guy Fawkes laying the fuse

CHAPTER I

LONDON

1605

IN November 1605 a group of Catholics attempted to blow up King James I at the opening of Parliament. When James I came down from Scotland to succeed to the throne in 1604 he declared himself in favour of the laws against Catholics. As a result the plot was hatched. A house was rented next to the Houses of Parliament in May 1604, but the opening of Parliament was postponed until February 1605. Tunnelling under the House of Lords from the rented house started in December. One of the conspirators, Guy Fawkes, kept watch and for two weeks none of his comrades appeared above ground. Their nerve must have been stretched almost to breaking point when they heard that the opening of Parliament had been postponed yet again and set for 5th November 1605. In March of that year a cellar under the Peer's Chamber became available and so, after all their hard labour, the tunnel was abandoned. Under the cover of darkness, thirty-six barrels of gunpowder were ferried across the Thames and placed in position.

The conspirators dispersed for the summer and agreed to induce their friends in Parliament to avoid the opening without actually giving the plot away. One of the plotters, however, sent an ambiguous letter to his brother-in-law, Lord Monteagle, warning of 'a terrible blow'. When the others heard of the letter they made plans to leave London at short notice, but Guy Fawkes decided to keep watch over the powder. On 4th November he was in the cellar when it was searched but the officers, although discovering the barrels of gunpowder, left. Fawkes, hiding in the corner, escaped detection and decided to warn his comrades, but when he returned to the cellar at midnight on 5th November he was arrested. He declared that had he been in the cellar when the search party came he would have 'blown him up, house, himself and all'.

The King was called from his bed. Guy Fawkes calmly told him that a desperate disease required a desperate remedy, and that 'one of his objects was to blow the Scots back again into Scotland'. Fawkes then endured three days of horrific torture on the rack, giving his comrades time to escape before releasing their names. But it was no use. Four were killed resisting arrest and eight others, including Guy Fawkes, were tried at Westminster Hall in January. They were drawn to the scaffold on sleds and after being hanged their heads were cut off and displayed on poles. The last to die was Guy Fawkes, so weak from torture that he could hardly climb the ladder to the scaffold.

Thus ended one of 'the greatest treasons that ever were plotted in England' as the Attorney General described it. Thus, also, began one of the most popular and enduring of English traditions. To be on the safe side Parliament was thereafter searched before each opening of Parliament and this still happens with full ceremony. The Fifth of November has been celebrated ever since with bonfires, fireworks and effigies of Guy Fawkes in ways that can be both lively and weird. Of all the celebrations that have taken place over the last four centuries, however, those in Victorian Guildford must rank amongst the strangest.

CHAPTER II

HENRY PEAK MEETS THE GUYS

1851

I N 1851 Henry Peak came to live in Guildford. He was nineteen and had left his parents in London to pursue a career as an architect and surveyor. There was much to discover about Guildford but nothing compared with the astonishing way in which Guildfordians celebrated 5th November. Many years later Peak recorded in his journal his first encounter with the Guildford Guys:

> I had, of course, heard something of the lively doings which might be expected and in London . . . there were celebrations, in which like others I had been pleased to participate, with fireworks and bonfires to commemorate the doings of 'Guy Fawkes' but they were in a very tame and small way, in comparison with the doings at Guildford, and I certainly was not prepared for the scene which was enacted.

> On the day in question I had been very busily employed in the office, and had not been out until I left the Portsmouth Road rather late in the evening to go to my lodging, and upon crossing the bridge a surprising spectacle presented itself: — there in the distance, at the steps in the roadway opposite Trinity Church, a great fire was burning, brilliantly lighting up all around, and the whole town was as if in a state of siege; every shop window not protected with shutters, and other exposed glass on the ground floor of houses, was barricaded; and wet straw and manure heaped . . . to prevent the penetration of fireworks; for as I found these were formidable and dangerous things — being

Holy Trinity Church

immense squibs many of them 12 or 15 inches in length and 1 ½ and 2 inches in diameter, and being chiefly loaded with gunpowder, and heavily rammed, their force of explosion when discharged was tremendous, and notwithstanding the precautions, I saw several mount to a great height, and some eventually entered the upper windows of the houses, so that there was danger to life and limb both in and out, and also of fire to the buildings, and everyone had to be on the alert to act in case of necessity.

As to myself, I had letters to post, and then curiosity drew me closer towards the fire, where a great and lawless crowd was gathered; the chiefs who were fantastically dressed in various costumes, were members of the 'Guy's Society', an organised body defying the police and officials of the town, and a saturnalia of mob rule was being carried on for the time being. Indeed the whole place was at the mercy of the 'Guys', who gave orders to the mob by means of a horn, the blasts of which were understood and acted upon accordingly; and so the 'Guys' and their followers would sally forth from time to time for 'plunder', and return laden with spoil of pales of fences, gates, doors and anything which spite or fancy prompted them to make a raid upon and these were cast upon the fire with shouting and noisy demonstrations.

This eerie and sinister scene had all the hallmarks of a protest but it was, in fact, the traditional way in which Guildfordians celebrated Bonfire Night. For many locals 5th November was one of the most exciting nights of the year. One regular participant was John Mason. Unlike Henry Peak he was a true local, born and brought up in Guildford, as were his father and his grandfather. Along with other boys, he had spent the autumn evenings of his childhood making squibs in the cellar of a house in Mount Street. They clubbed together to purchase gunpowder from the gunpowder works at Chilworth. When Mason grew up and took over his father's carpentry business he inherited the responsibility of barricading vulnerable properties on the Fifth and removing the protection the following day. He found it easy to justify the behaviour of the Bonfire Night revellers: 'Guildford boys', he wrote, 'were born with the uncontrollable habit of celebrating Guy Fawkes Day in the way their fathers had done. To non-Guildfordians this savoured of insubordination — the papers in some cases even calling the proceedings riotous! This was not intended when I took part in it — it simply meant keeping up an old custom handed down for generations'.

Another local recorded the festivities with tremendous enthusiasm:

> Much led up to it. The making of squib cases, the display of masks in the shop windows, the mystery of mixing gunpowder and iron dust which Lymposs's smiths [a smithy in upper High Street] were good enough to give to any boy who asked civilly for some, the operation of making of touchpaper out of old copies of the 'West Surrey' and saltpetre, all this did a lot to give interest to what was otherwise a dull time. School on the afternoon of the Fifth was apt to be an unreality, and in the rush home one noticed that . . . stable manure was being put down lavishly

over people's iron gratings (one old lady living in the High Street hung a cotton apron across her cellar window to keep out the squibs), carpenters were busy boarding up fanlights, and as everyone knew everyone else, one could easily detect a few athletic-looking strangers about, looking particularly unconcerned. They came from Aldershot Camp, and at the White Lion or elsewhere every man has a bag with his disguise and a supply of fireworks to tuck up under his blouse. An intense feeling of expectancy runs through the town. Which way would the Guys come, by way of the Mount, or down 'one of the roads'? Nobody knew until the deep-throated war cry roared through the street, and peaceful folk fled as for their lives. 'Phill-a-loo Muster', with a great stress on the 'Mus', is what it sounded like. The Guys had come.

Very few minutes sufficed to start the fire in front of the church and the fun began. How the flames shot up and made the church tower stand out in bright red and deep shade! The front of Abbot's Hospital glittered with the reflection from the open casement windows, where the white faces of the inmates peered out from a safe distance. Boys climbed the stone balustrade and twined their bodies round the iron arch over the entrance gate, and one wondered, looking on from the church steps, whether they were living beings or statues. The churchyard terrace was a sanctuary, by the common consent, for women and children, and rarely a squib or a cracker went that way of set purpose.

Not everyone shared this enthusiasm. Many people were as horrified as Peak. On 11th November 1851, a few days after Peak encountered the Guys, he was able to read an article in the *Sussex Advertiser* which heavily criticised the event. It no doubt represented the views of many people when it complained:

The proceedings were really disgraceful; you never saw such an affair in your life. The mob were suffered to do just as they pleased . . . .What our magistrates can be thinking about I cannot conceive. It would appear that they don't think at all . . . We trust that for the future the magistrates will be alive to their duty, and prove that the law is still strong enough to reach these parties, spite their combination . . . .We sincerely hope that this will be the last time on which we shall have occasion to complain of these scandalous proceedings.

There were even rumours that members of the Town Council actively supported the mob. But whatever the truth the authorities were in a very difficult position. They had only three policemen under their command and given the strong support for the bonfire it must have been hard to decide the best course of action. The simplest solution was to compromise. The authorities made a token effort towards maintaining the law, but were reluctant to antagonise the Guys. On 6th November 1843, for example, P.C. High warned a Guy in the Queen's Head: 'Don't be too fast. I have orders for you to let [fireworks] . . . off if you keep out of mischief.'

But mischief did occur. Later that evening Superintendent Hollington had his hat knocked off as he and some constables approached a fire in Mount Street. They broke through the crowd surrounding the flames and kicked out the fire but the Guys were too strong. As the police walked back down the hill they were pelted with stones and fireworks. Scuffles broke out and several policemen were injured. Two Guys were convicted but refused to pay their fines in protest. When they were sentenced to gaol, their supporters paid the fines and paraded the men round the town with a band.

Year after year it was a similar story. The authorities failed to come up with a means of suppressing the disturbances. The police were knocked about if they interfered and no one was successfully punished. This gave the *Sussex Advertiser* plenty to moan about. On 10th November 1846 it wrote: 'We can but participate in the wonder felt and expressed by the more respectable portions of the inhabitants, that no active measures at all commensurate with the evil, are taken by the authorities, to put down these yearly orgies. We suppose it will go on . . . till someone is killed or some extensive damage be done to the property of some of the authorities themselves'. The following year (9th November 1847) it complained: 'It is very odd, but young men who would repel the charge of dishonesty with scorn . . . seem to think there is not the least harm in wilfully robbing peaceable citizens of their property for the purpose of making a bonfire'.

The problem was not new, nor was it confined to Guildford. Similar incidents took place in towns and villages all over southern England — Chelmsford, Exeter, Rye, Godalming, Horsham, Brighton and Lewes to name a few. Lewes is still famous for these kinds of celebrations and was also notorious in 1851. The *Sussex Advertiser* bemoaned that the streets in that year, 'were, as is, alas!, usual on this anniversary, the scene of uninterrupted disorder and riot . . . .Towards nine o'clock there was a general union of forces in the High Street. Here the discharge of rockets &c was incessant; lighted tar barrels were dragged through the streets by the usual mob, and a large bonfire was lighted opposite the County Hall'.

Bonfire Night had a long tradition behind it. The story of Guy Fawkes's part in a Catholic plot to blow up the King and Parliament was well known. Everyone knew how he was caught red-handed when the cellars were searched. The deliverance gave those in power much to celebrate, and James I proclaimed that his day of deliverance should be remembered with thanksgiving in the churches. The Book of Common Prayer used to contain appropriate prayers and the *Illustrated London News* in 1850 mentioned several London churches which held special services with sermons.

This official encouragement must have been one of the reasons why 5th November became established as a festival. In the eighteenth century the Guildford authorities did their bit to keep the occasion alive. In 1704 and 1706 the Mayor's accounts refer to 'wine on Gunpowder treason'.

There were bonfires and fireworks on other occasions as well. In 1756 Admiral Blakeney, who defended Minorca in the Seven

Years War passed through Guildford and his success was celebrated with a bonfire and illuminations.

There were, however, indications that trouble could occur. The burning of Guy Fawkes effigies was harmless enough but it became more sinister when representations of unpopular contemporaries were set alight. Admiral Byng, for example, had failed to relieve Minorca and so, when he passed through the town, his effigy was burnt on the steps of Holy Trinity. In 1774 the Reverend Cole was enjoying his boiled chicken in the White Hart (now Sainsbury's) when he saw a riotous mob outside the window burning two effigies of unpopular tradesmen.

In the years following the French Revolution, town authorities became wary of encouraging mobs to take to the streets. They

Guy Fawkes Celebrations, 1808

followed the example of London where fireworks were being banned in open places due to the risk of fires and drunken brawls. In Guildford the authorities initially tried to confine fireworks to special occasions such as the Peace of Amiens in 1802 or the victory at Trafalgar in 1805. After 1805, however, they decided it would be wise to ban fireworks completely. In 1809, the country was ordered to celebrate George III's Golden Jubilee. A meeting of Guildford inhabitants was convened by the Mayor and it was decided to hold a thanksgiving service. There were, however, to be no illuminations, fireworks or bonfires, 'the first of which causes a useless waste of money (which might be applied to a better purpose) and the whole tends to create Tumult and Disorder'.

But it was not easy to stop a centuries old tradition. In 1828 a disturbing plot was only just foiled as an account written in that year reveals:

> On November 5th 1827, a great deal of damage and mischief was done in the Town of Guildford by Persons letting off Fireworks for which informations were laid against several individuals who were convicted and fined in the full penalty of Five Pounds imposed by a local Act of Parliament since which time there has been a very malicious and hostile feeling on the part of those fined both against the Persons who informed against them and the magistrates who convicted them. On the 5th of November instant to prevent the same damage occurring again the Mayor and Magistrates determined to prevent and put a stop to the Fireworks in the Town altogether of which intention they gave notice and they with the Constables and Peace Officers paraded the streets nearly the whole night and effectively suppressed the nuisance.

> The Town of Guildford is lighted with Gas and the Gas Works is situated at the lower end of the town. Several young men conspired together to extinguish the Gas Lights for the purpose it is believed to defeat the intentions and measures of the Mayor and Magistrates, to create a riot if it had fully succeeded (the night being very dark) as it would then have been impossible to have recognised the parties engaged.

The keeper of the Gas House was at home on 5th November when at 7.30pm his light went out. He hurried to the Gas House to find that the main valve had been turned off, and was just in time to prevent the whole town from being plunged into darkness. Three men were suspected but there was insufficient evidence to prosecute.

It is not known when the Guys first appeared and 5th November took on the form discovered by Henry Peak. It does seem clear, however, that the Guys societies were formed in towns to keep Bonfire Night alive at a time when town authorities were withdrawing their support and becoming hostile to celebrations. It would also seem that the troubles in Guildford on 5th November were escalating in the decade before Henry Peak's arrival. In 1850 the *Illustrated London News* stated that 5th November was a neglected event but, 'The recent revival by the Pope of the Roman Catholic Episcopacy in this country which has excited so much indignation amongst the clergy and the laity, has had the effect of giving quite a new character to the — of late years — almost forgotten anniversary of Gunpowder Plot'. The Papacy decided in 1850 to re-introduce the administrative system of bishops and dioceses abolished at the Reformation. It was a purely practical measure to help the Catholic Church cope with the growing numbers of Catholics in England but it aroused strong anti-Catholic feeling amongst fervent Protestants. Peak recalled how the streets of London that year were full of effigies of the Pope, Cardinals and Priests. According to the *Illustrated London News* slogans were whitewashed on walls saying 'No Popery', 'No wafer gods!', 'No Catholic humbug'. A great procession marched through the centre of London carrying the effigies including a 16-foot-high Guy Fawkes. Anti-Catholic feeling was not obvious in the Guildford celebrations, but there are other indications that the situation witnessed by Peak emerged in the 1840s. In 1843 Mr Edward Vincent defending one of the Guys in court, recalled that although fireworks were forbidden every year no one had been prosecuted for fourteen or fifteen years and implied that the attempts to punish the Guys were a new departure for the authorities. In 1844 the bonfire was lit outside Holy Trinity for the first time on that spot in eight years.

What lay behind all this strange behaviour? To a certain extent fireworks and bonfires encourage mischief. Even modern firework parties can make respectable people behave recklessly. Although Henry Peak frowned upon the events he witnessed in Guildford he was not above getting a thrill out of gunpowder, treason and plot: 'I think that the reddest of red-letter days to the boys of London was the Fifth of November; its celebration coming as it did when the days were dull and the evenings were long, and commemorating an event which stirred the minds of all who really thought about it . . . .There were bonfires, fireworks, effigies intended to represent Guy Fawkes, being carried through the streets during the day time with the object of collecting money to pay for the fireworks at night'. Mischief did take place. On several occasions Irish Catholics employed at a paper-staining factory near Peak's home went on the rampage, destroying the effigies that young boys had spent weeks making. But still the troubles in Guildford and other southern rural towns had a character of their own. To see them in perspective we need to understand the people who took part and so we must now turn our attention to Guildford in 1851.

CHAPTER III

GUILDFORD IN 1851

IF you go to the bottom of Guildford High Street, across the river and up the Mount you come to a delightful open space called Guildown. Displayed before you is a panorama of north Surrey dominated by Guildford Cathedral on Stag Hill. It is a lovely view but one is forced to recognise how built up Surrey has become. When Henry Peak came to Guildford in 1851 there was hardly anything to see but countryside. A book of rambles published in 1850 described how one could look from Guildown across cornfields and odd patches of trees. Here and there were the country houses of gentlemen, farms and church steeples peeping out above the foliage. The only buildings between Guildown and the railway lines were those belonging to a few farms. To the far right of our view Guildford was a fraction of its modern size. To the north of the town Woodbridge Road ran through fields. Stoke Church stood alone with Stoke Mansion surrounded by Stoke Park. To the east, Charlotteville was still to be built and the town did not spread farther south than the castle.

The whole town nestled comfortably into the gap in the North Downs and Henry Peak thought it was delightful. Its beautiful position could be seen clearly from the train that brought him to Guildford early one February morning in 1851. He obtained his first proper look of his new home from the bridge at the bottom of the High Street. The river was high that day and the water rolling under the bridge made the scene appear even more impressive.

The steep High Street clearly displayed its collection of picturesque buildings with their gables, bay windows and beautiful brickwork. The Town Hall (known as the Guildhall) stood out prominently with its bell turret and ornamented clock dial. Even the relatively new Corn Market (now Tunsgate), built in 1818 seemed to add interest to the street. Peak loved all the old buildings — the churches, Abbot's Hospital, the Grammar School and the castle ruins. He recalled:

> I felt too that the town had such a cheery and busy aspect and that so much was continually going on. The Corn Market on Saturdays was a scene of much interest and activity. What a throng of farmers and dealers from the country round occupied the market and roadway thereabouts . . . . The weekly cattle and pig markets were also a novelty to me, held as they were in the open streets (High Street and Market Street) — as were the crowded sheep and cattle fairs in May and November, which were scenes impressed upon one's memory; with the motley gatherings of the so called pleasure fairs, held when the cattle business was ended. What an array there then was, of booths and ginger bread stalls with the shows and roundabouts and the like in the wider space by Holy Trinity . . . . Then in October came round the ancient chartered fair at St Catherine's. A never-to-be-forgotten wild and weird scene it was . . . . The booths and shows and stalls being arranged up and along the steep hill-side, and hubbub and noise reigning supreme. I visited the fair in the evening, the first year of my being at Guildford . . . to view the peculiar and picturesque assembly.

Henry Peak's picture of the town was obviously one sided but it reminds us of how different the place was. It was not yet a base for thousands of commuters or even an attractive shopping centre. Its main function was to serve as a market centre for the goods brought in from the surrounding farms. Compared with today's town it was not without its attractions. There were no large offices destroying the views of the town; no cars crowding the streets and polluting the air with noise and fumes. For the better off it was an elegant age in which ladies wore flowing crinoline dresses and men

Guildford from Mount Pleasant

walked around the town in top hats. They lived with their servants either in the country houses round the town or in large town houses, and there were many respectable pursuits for them to enjoy. One fine July day in 1851 Mr Haydon opened his garden in Millmead House to members of the Horticultural Society. To the strains of the town's brass band guests strolled amongst the trees admiring the flower displays and making polite conversation. Other amenities in the town included the Public Hall where the Guildford Choral Society gave concerts, and where learned citizens gave public lectures on subjects such as 'The Formation of the Earth' or 'Politics and Christianity'. There was also a theatre in Market Street offering plays at irregular intervals. So there was a middle class society in Guildford but the town was not yet the respectable bastion it is today. Guildford remained for the time being a rural market town inhabited mainly by shopkeepers, craftsmen and labourers and visited by farm workers. Most Guildfordians had more in common with the carpenter John Mason than with the members of the Horticultural Society.

In 1851 John Mason was living with his wife in Bury Street. They had been married for just two years. The ceremony had taken place in St Clement Danes in London but there had been no honeymoon. The couple came straight home to an empty and dilapidated old house with a blacksmith's shop attached. Trying to make it comfortable was a nightmare. Mason often came home from work to find his wife in tears after her inability to clean the brick floor or some other piece of housework.

It was common for wives to stay at home during the day-time. The 1851 census shows that most women in Guildford had either no professional occupation or helped their husbands with their businesses. The minority who were employed tended to be teachers, governesses or servants or to be involved with making or repairing clothing. Mason remembered that his mother's life was one of unending toil. There were no servants and she spent all her time baking, brewing and washing. As well as Mason and his two sisters to care for there was a pig to fatten up. Pigs were a part of family life for many people in this period. Butcher's meat was considered a luxury and so these poor animals were fattened and slaughtered mercilessly in the cold weather. Their squeals were often heard early in the morning as the pig-sticker went to work in the lanes leading off the High Street. Boys rushed to the scene to enjoy the warmth of the fire used to burn off the hairs. The pettitoes were pulled from the feet and cast amongst the children. Less well-off families in the town and countryside relied on their pigs to provide them with most of their meat in the winter, and the pig's death was often cause for celebration. So as well as the attractions described by Peak there was a less pleasant side to life in Guildford. Even the cheery markets he described seem less pleasant when one thinks of the smell and noise of the animals and the dust they churned up which entered the houses along the High Street.

Family life was regularly affected with the pain of bereavement. In Britain a third of the children born failed to reach the age of twenty and only half lived into their forties. In 1849 Reverend J.C. Cox wrote 'A Few Words to the Inhabitants of Guildford on the Sanitary Condition of their Town' declaring that bad drains and a restricted water supply led to typhus, cholera, consumption and other diseases among the poor, who were huddled in over-crowded and insanitary conditions in the gates and tenements leading off the High Street. There was little time for leisure and few outlets for entertainment. The first holiday John Mason had with his wife was in 1851 when they spent a day in London and battled with the crowds at the Great Exhibition in Hyde Park.

The Guildford Institute offered working men the opportunity to improve their education but the main source of entertainment for many working men was the local pub. Throughout most of the nineteenth century there were over thirty public houses in the High Street alone. The local newspaper regularly reported tales of agricultural workers who were found late at night in the street, sleeping off the effects of their evening out. The public house provided one of the few places in which men could meet their friends. Their wives stayed at home with the children and socialised by visiting each other's homes.

For those living in the countryside life could also be hard and the opportunities for enjoyment were equally limited. Surrey was still a land of farms, with some industry as Kelly's *Surrey* explained in 1855:

> The county, is on the whole, an unfavourable one for agriculture; but on the rivers are rich market gardens, producing asparagus and peas, while a good deal of corn, hops and grass are produced. Farnham is great hop country. On the Downs many sheep are fed. A good deal of coppice wood and timber is planted . . . .

> The manufactures in the metropolitan suburbs are extensive and various. On the mill-streams many factories are also estab-

lished, and the shire has long held a respectable manufacturing rank. The calico bleaching and printing, once carried on upon the Wandle is a good deal fallen off but snuff, drug and copper mills are still extensive. Brush and broom making is a considerable business, also paper making and malting. Brick making, glass working, cement working and pottery form another branch of business.

The census provides a picture of the people who lived round Guildford in 1851. In West End Tithing (approximately modern Wood Street about three miles north-west of Guildford) there were 544 people living in 109 households. About three-quarters of the heads of families were farmers or agricultural labourers. Many of the others were heavily involved with the farming community as blacksmiths, carpenters, sawyers and wheelwrights. Only eighty-four people were born outside Surrey and most people were born locally in the parish of Worplesdon. In her book *Old West Surrey,* Gertrude Jekyll wrote about the country life in mid-nineteenth century Surrey. Her description is a reminder that Guildfordians of the Victorian age cannot be judged by modern standards.

> Their lives have been perhaps all the happier in that they have been concerned with few wants and few responsibilities; and if their thoughts are mainly of haytime and harvest, and root-crops, and the care of sheep and cattle, shall we presume to think that these interests are of less account than our own; for, after all, what can be of greater need or of more supreme importance?

HIGH-STREET, GUILDFORD, LOOKING WEST.

The daily life of the cottager varied so little in one cottage or another, or in one village or the next, that the usual restriction of ideas and interests was only to be expected . . . . The farmers were very strict about men coming to their time in the morning. If a man came late he lost a quarter of a day's pay; very likely he was told he was not wanted at all that day . . . . They worked long hours in those old days, children and all. Children of six and seven years of age were employed on the farms, just as they had been fifty years before . . . . Children had not so much playtime in the older days but girls had more than boys . . . . Mothers of labourers' families were glad to get their girls out at an early age into any respectable family where they would be fed in return for their work. One old woman I knew told me that she went out at the age of twelve.

'It was a carpenter's family', she said, 'and there was eleven children. Yes that was my first place, for a year. I didn't get no wages, only my food, one frock and one bonnet, and a shillin' to take home. Then I was hired for a year to go to a farm where the master was a widower, and after that at another farm where there was two ladies. They was the particularest ladies I ever knowd. It ud do any girl good to go and live with such as they. There was the oak stairs — it was always a clean pail of water to every two steps; and I'd as much pride in it as they had. My wages never got as fur as four pound. Best place I ever lived in was at Mr. Woods's at Hambledon. Quietest and best master I ever lived with. There was the red-brick kitchen-floor. I use to flow he down with a green broom; best of brooms for bricks; makes the floors red. You makes 'em of the green broom as grows on the common. After I left, there was always a bit of green holly at Christmas, and any win'fall apples he always give me. Ah! he was a good master. He minded me when I was married, and time and again he sent me a bit of beef till he died — and then my beef died. One farm I lived in was nigh some rough ground where tramp people lived, and my missis used to send me out with beautiful gruel to the tramp women in the tents when there was a baby come'.

The village inn or ale-house was naturally the centre of gossip and general entertainment. When news travelled slowly and there were no cheap newspapers, and but few of the people could read or write, it was the only warm, cheerful place where men could meet and hear or exchange news.

GUILDFORD CASTLE.

In these circumstances it is not surprising that people looked forward to 5th November. It offered a rare night of excitement for people whose lives could be dull and often hard. Although the style of the Bonfire Night celebrations seems strange to modern minds it was in keeping with the customs and beliefs of rural west Surrey in the nineteenth century. Gertrude Jekyll recalled:

> Some kind of belief in witchcraft certainly existed among labouring people, at any rate, up to the middle of the nineteenth century. I can well remember how often we used to hear about it when I was a child.
>
> An old custom that I remember in my young days, as a strong expression of public opinion, was the performance of 'Rough music'. If a man was known to beat his wife, he was first warned. The warning was a quiet one enough — not a word was spoken; but someone went at night with a bag of chaff, and laid a train of it from the roadway up to the cottage door. It meant, 'We know that thrashing is going on here'. If the man took the hint and treated his wife better, nothing more happened. But if the ill-treatment went on, a number of men and boys came some other night with kettles and pans and fire-irons, and anything they could lay their hands on to make a noise with, and gave him 'Rough music'. The din was something dreadful, but the effect was said to be salutary. My home was half a mile from the village, but every now and then on summer nights we used to hear the discordant strains of this orchestra of public protest and indignation.

When Guildfordians enjoyed themselves they insisted in being rather boisterous with it. Mason commented, 'Upon various occasions and for different reasons . . . crowds of people gathered together in the town and when this happened it would invariably terminate in a fight . . . .Were men more pugnacious in those days?' Take as an example the fair at St Catherine's which Peak described as a wild and weird affair. Each year there was a traditional fight before the fair, during which the locals pelted passers-by with chestnuts. One year, John Mason recalled, a real battle took place when the fair became infested with swindlers using cups known as 'thimble riggers'. The annoyed Guildfordians took the matter into their own hands and in a vicious battle, with injuries on both sides they drove the 'thimble riggers' across the river.

Thus the lifestyle of Guildfordians helps us appreciate their strange behaviour on Bonfire Night. In the same way, the attitude of the town authorities towards the Guys becomes more understandable when one looks at how the town was run. In 1851 the local authority was not the great provider it has since become. Town councils were traditionally concerned with overseeing the properties and incomes of the town, regulating trading practices and maintaining order. Their functions did not stretch to the provision of a wide range of services. This meant that as towns grew in the eighteenth century there was no official body to tackle the social problems that arose. Concerned individuals tended to band together and established bodies by private Acts of Parliament to supervise tasks such as paving, lighting, police or drainage. These bodies did not always provide an efficient service and many jobs now performed by the Borough or County Council were the responsibility of householders.

Guildfordians were responsible under a local paving act for sweeping outside the fronts of their houses. They also had to water the streets in hot weather to prevent the dust from blowing about. A water cart toured the town to wet the roads but in 1851 it did not go round until the end of the summer. Minor streets were lit at night by oil lamps on wooden poles but more and more streets were being lit by gas supplied by the Guildford Gas and Coke Company. Gas was introduced to the town in 1824 and a gasometer was erected in the Farnham Road. The service provided, however, was far from satisfactory. At a meeting at the Town Hall in September 1851 the councillors complained about the enormous amount of money consumers paid for a very poor gas supply. The gas was of such a poor quality that the pipes had to be cleaned out every couple of months and the street lamps gave off no more light than a candle. About six weeks before the meeting there had been no lights at all and a lamp at the Abbot's Hospital had not worked for weeks. A guide to Guildford published in 1845 provided a possible explanation for the inefficiency of the gas company. It explained that 'from accidental circumstances great expenses were incurred at the commencement of the undertaking and consequently the proprietors have hitherto realised little or no percentage'.

The fire precautions were another area where provision was alarmingly lacking. The town had two fire engines but did not provide a professional fire service. The engines were stored at the Town Hall and the Corn Market at Tunsgate and were operated by local blacksmiths. Russell's *Almanack* for 1853 explained that Number Two Fire Engine could not be taken more than seven miles from Guildford without the consent of the Mayor. The engineer had to be paid twenty shillings and the firemen seven shillings. Any damage to hoses, buckets and the engine had to be paid for. To add to the inconvenience, the fire engines, buckets and ladders were all kept in different buildings. Once the equipment had been brought together there was still the problem of finding a supply of water. In June 1851 a fire broke out at a shop in Spital Street (now Upper High Street) when embers in a bacon store ignited some sawdust. Neighbours and the police were quickly on the scene but for over an hour after the fire was discovered there was no water in the mains for the fire engine to use. Fortunately the landlord of the George Inn had a tank of water in his yard capable of holding 1000 gallons and a small engine was able to use this to extinguish the fire.

The water was apparently turned off at night to avoid the danger of flooding from leaking pipes when everyone was asleep. This meant that when water was needed for the fire engine the public officer responsible for water had to be fetched from his home. Mr Hooke, the officer in question, went to the waterworks to turn on the supply. According to the newspaper account of the incident there was a plug at the bottom of Tunsgate for turning the water up or down the town as required. Mr Hooke, however, decided that since he was barely clad he would go home and put on some more clothes before checking the plug. The key to the plug was held at the police station in Tunsgate and when he arrived there he found that the key had gone. He assumed someone else had used it and hearing from a few people that the fire was out it seems he went home to bed. For a man whose role was crucial to the operation of the fire engine his attitude was very relaxed and not surprisingly he was censured for his behaviour.

At the public meeting held to discuss the fire, complaints about the water supply were voiced. Not all houses were supplied with an adequate supply and a Mr Higgasson complained that he had been without water for several days. When he 'sent to complain of the circumstances he had not the most pleasant of answers sent back'. Perhaps one of the problems was that Mr Hooke was overstretched; according to John Mason, he was the agent for the gas company as well as the water company. On top of that he ran a plumbers, painters and glaziers business and was choirmaster and organist at Shalford Church.

The water company was originally set up in 1701 by a Mr Yarnold, who obtained a grant from the Mayor and Approved Men. In 1845 there were eight shares in the company. Three were held by the Town Corporation and the rest by individuals. The reservoir was on Pewley Hill and water was raised 100 feet from the river by an engine at the mill dam in Millmead.

Emergencies requiring medical aid relied on the efforts of local doctors. Injured people were taken to a nearby house while a doctor was fetched. The nearest hospital was in London. In October 1851 a railway worker was badly hurt at Guildford Station, and he was taken up to Waterloo and then to St Thomas's Hospital due to the lack of local provision.

It was not that Guildfordians cared little for their town. They were just reluctant to spend money. In October 1851, at a meeting of the Liberals, a Mr Chennel was greeted with cheers when he said they ought to send to the council people who would 'study economy'.

It is easy to laugh at the poor organisation revealed by these anecdotes but it is important to remember the annoyance and hardship the situation must have caused. We must resist the temptation of conjuring up a nostalgic picture of the town and a good way of redressing the balance is by looking at one of the most sinister aspects of Victorian England: the workhouse. This institution has done much to colour our view of the Victorians but it can also provide an insight into their attitudes.

In the early nineteenth century there were two main systems of relief for the poor — the workhouse and outdoor relief provided by the parish under the 1601 Elizabethan Poor Law. Little is known about the Guildford Workhouse in Millmead but John Mason has provided us with a brief glimpse of the operation of outdoor relief, his father being one of the relieving officers. Mason wrote, 'I have seen men and women come to the house as vagrants and receive such relief as on questioning them he thought they ought to have'. There were also some private local charities providing relief of which the most famous was the Abbot's Hospital which provided almshouses for the elderly.

Workhouses generally had an appalling reputation. The able bodied, poor, sick and insane were jumbled together. The system of outdoor relief was also criticised by those who believed it encouraged the poor to be a burden on the rates instead of finding work. In 1832 the government appointed a Royal Commission to investigate the operation of the Poor Laws, and out of this came the Poor Law Amendment Act of 1834. Parishes were grouped together into 600 Poor Law unions run by locally elected guardians who were responsible to the Poor Law Commission. (The Commission was converted in 1847 to the Poor Law Board. The president of the Board sat in Parliament and on the Cabinet.) Hence policy was decided nationally and administered locally, and in many ways the new system was an improvement on previous practice. Cleanliness, at least, was insisted upon in the workhouses. However, in its single-minded determination to prevent the poor from exploiting the parish rates, the Act abolished outdoor relief wherever possible. Furthermore, in order to discourage the poor from being a burden by entering the workhouse, conditions were made as unpleasant as possible without being unhealthy. The diet was spartan, discipline harsh, the sexes were separated and the work was hard, tedious and undignified. Critics claimed the system dealt with the symptoms and not the causes of poverty but, in fairness to the Victorians, there was no solution at the time. It had to await further industrial and administrative growth. Even Dickens, who attacked the system in *Oliver Twist* did not propose a solution.

Guildford sold its old workhouse in 1837 and built a new one the following year on the site of the modern St Luke's Hospital. A guide to Guildford published in 1845 provides a very interesting description of the workhouse. The attitude of the author is very illuminating for he betrays mixed feelings about the place. He optimistically hopes that the best is being done for the poor but expresses regret and pity for some of the people he saw there.

GUILDFORD UNION WORKHOUSE

Under the provisions of the New Poor Law Amendment Act, a spacious and commodious workhouse has been erected on an elevated spot adjoining the Epsom Road. The building is . . . approved by the Commissioners, and is so contrived so as to admit the usual advantages of classification and separation. The six grand divisions are those of able-bodied paupers, male and female, the aged of both sexes, and the boys and girls, who are educated, under resident instructors within the walls. Separate work-rooms, day rooms and sleeping apartments, are allotted to each class and the discipline is, necessarily, of the strictest cast . . . .A comfortable and healthy temperature is kept during cold weather, in all the rooms . . . .There is a powerful bone crushing mill, worked by cranks, from the able-bodied male class yard . . . .There is a large return of cash for bone dust, but the trade is more beneficial in finding occupation for the inmates, than for the sake of profit obtained. The poor in the neighbourhood, however, find a source of advantage, in the circumstance of their children collecting bones which were heretofore wasted.

Guildford Union Workhouse

The union itself comprises of twenty parishes . . . .Guardians are elected from each parish, and, with the magistrates of the division, form a board, whose periodical meetings are held at the house every Saturday . . . .The board have the power of making by-laws, at their own discretion, and in them is vested the appointment of the various officers of the union. These comprise a clerk or secretary, . . . an auditor . . . [and] . . . two relieving officers. [There was also a governor, matron, superintendent, porter, chaplain and other subordinate assistants.]

The schools [in the workhouse] may be considered the most interesting portions of the establishment, since, in a measure they recognise the principle that the duty of the board is to prevent, and not foster the evil of pauperism. The boys are instructed in the orthography and construction of the English language, writing and the three first rules of arithmetic, and in the rudiments of geography, history and other branches of knowledge by a resident schoolmaster (Mr Ames) . . . .

The Girls school is conducted by Miss Ames . . . .The instruction is chiefly confined to reading, writing, and needlework, while the elder girls are employed in the various household duties of the establishment. Thus initiated and prepared, they are constantly sought out, removed into respectable service, and, with very few exceptions, have done credit to the moral culture they have received.

There is an infirmary at the rear of the premises where every attention is bestowed on the sick . . . .No disorder of an infectious nature has ever been engendered within the walls.

The able-bodied paupers are principally employed at the bone-mill. The women are engaged in washing, needlework, and the usual duties of the house. The class of inmates that more particularly excite commiseration are those whom age and infirmity, after years of industrious exertion, have incapacitated for further labour. These, however, enjoy some slight privileges, and partake of a few insignificant luxuries. Of the latter the article of tea is, to the female portion, the most important; and we envy not the feeling of the political economist who would deprive them of the

solace of the grateful and cheerful beverage. Yet, to witness a
hoary and years-stricken man, in such an establishment, is
calculated to give a sad shock to the better feelings of our nature.

In one sense the Poor Law Amendment Act marked a new era
in local provision in which policy was decided on a national level.
The year 1835 saw a turning point in Guildford's history for in
that year the Municipal Corporations Act was passed and the
Mayor and Approved Men of Guildford were replaced with an
elected Borough Council. The Approved Men had not been elected
but had co-opted new members on as vacancies arose. They
provided few services and acted largely as magistrates. Borough
rates were rarely levied and most of the Corporations income was
derived from market tolls. The Municipal Corporations Act
changed all this. It established local authorities that were account-
able to the electorate and upon which Parliament could bestow
certain responsibilities. The new corporations took over corporate
property, were empowered to provide street lighting and forced to
set up police forces. Otherwise their powers were limited but in
the years that followed they were authorised to set up museums,
public libraries and baths and to provide many other services now
associated with municipal government.

The inhabitants of Guildford did not however wait for legislation.
They frequently campaigned for better services. In June 1851 the
gas consumers met at the White Lion Hotel (now the White Lion
Walk) to discuss ways of getting better and cheaper gas. Their
protests were not in vain for on 14th October the *Surrey Gazette*
reported that the company was reducing its prices in the face of
public dissatisfaction. The new prices may have influenced a thinly
attended public meeting which discussed putting street lighting in
Chertsey Street and Stoke Road. Gas was chosen because it was
cheaper than oil and work started on raising funds to lay pipes.
On the matter of drainage the Commissioners of Paving decided
to put all the open sewers underground. The farmers were also in
discussion. They wanted the market to be moved from the High
Street to a more convenient place near the centre of town. At a

meeting held to discuss the water supply, a motion was carried, 'That a committee be appointed to confer with the proprietors of the waterworks, and with the Town Council, for the purpose of instituting . . . a constant supply of water during the night, and the greatest facility of applying the engine with the least possible delay'.

The biggest change was brought about by the railway which reached Guildford from London in 1845 and proceeded down to Portsmouth. Four years later the Reading-Reigate line was completed. The arrival of the railway in Surrey's countryside made it possible for the wealthy to live farther out of London. On 2nd September the *Surrey Gazette* commented that in nearby Dorking attractive villa residences had been built which attracted the rich and boosted the town's economy. It argued that the same should happen in Guildford. The railway also gave Guildfordians the opportunity to travel. In 1851, as John Mason found out, the Great Exhibition in Hyde Park provided a marvellous, if tiring, excursion. Extra trains were put on to take the crowds up to London. The timetables were published in the *Surrey Gazette* and in October the paper reported that some trains carried 800 people and on one occasion the station was so packed that an accident was only just avoided.

This then was the town that faced the Guys each November. A short chapter such as this cannot hope to provide a comprehensive picture of the town, but it has aimed to put the Guy Riots in perspective. Guildford was very different from the town that exists today but it was also changing. Through the story of the Guy Riots we can see the impact that Victorian respectability and centralisation was to have on rural tradition.

CHAPTER IV

SOMETHING MUST BE DONE!

1852

THE Town Council had a problem. The gentlemen who met in the Council Room at the Guildhall had succeeded for years in tolerating the troubles on 5th November, but their attitude now had to change. In 1852 two of the Guys' victims decided to complain. One was the Reverend W. Walford of the 'Furze', London Road, the other was the Reverend Henry Shrubb of Braboeuf House, St Catherine's Hill. Both approached the town authorities for compensation. The Reverend Shrubb wrote:

> I beg to inform you that a most violent outrage was committed in this town last night on which the inhabitants have annually been accustomed to have a bonfire. In the evening a number of people amounting to several hundreds came into the town from the neighbouring villages, armed most of them with bludgeons, with their faces blackened and many men I believe in women's attire and about 10 o'clock they attacked my premises and forcibly took away about 50 yards of my oak . . . palings surrounding my garden leaving it exposed to the turnpike road and carrying them off to make their bonfire and for 2 or 3 hours they were employed in their outrageous proceedings. They threatened to murder my servant who was guarding the premises [who] could get no one to come to his assistance. Many of my neighbours I understand suffered in the same way. In short the whole town was for these 3 or 4 hours in a state of complete riot, with no one to oppose their lawless proceedings which were only termi-nated long after midnight by the men themselves being exhausted and worn out.

Town Hall, Guildford

The Borough Bench was very unsympathetic to the two clergymen when they asked for compensation. The magistrates said that
no one had warned the authorities about the possibility of a riot.
If in accordance with the Act of Parliament the Town Council had
been warned then it would have taken precautions. The clergymen
were not impressed by this rather pathetic excuse and took their
complaint further by writing to the Home Office. Once central
government was involved it was impossible for the authorities in
Guildford to ignore the situation. The Home Office asked for an
explanation and the Mayor, Mr Taylor, was full of excuses. He
started by explaining that it was impossible to take action:

> For nearly half a century scarcely a Fifth of November has
> gone over without some serious depredations to property here.
> Sometimes public meetings have been held to take measures for
> putting down the fireworks and bonfires and many of the inhabi-
> tants have been made special constables but who on interfering
> were overpowered by the mob. At other years prosecutions have
> been undertaken but the offenders generally escape punishment.
> Just previous to the last November 5th some discussion took
> place between some of the borough magistrates and the Chief
> Constable of the County Constabulary . . . as to the propriety of
> taking precautionary measures but it was concluded that as no
> great force could be spared from the towns and places of the
> county there was no chance of successfully opposing the mob.

Some of the rioters, he said, came from the surrounding villages
but the events were systematised by the inhabitants. In an attempt
to shift the blame away from the corporation, Taylor hinted that
the government did not provide enough support:

> I beg respectfully to communicate to you an opinion frequently
> expressed here that as many other places in England beside
> Guildford suffer in the same way from excesses on the Fifth of
> November there ought to be a legislative measure for giving
> injured parties a compensation at the charge of the borough rate
> in the boroughs. The small as well as large rate-payers in the
> boroughs would certainly then join in preventing the charge

falling on themselves. Rioters going about in their disguise should also be liable to a fine. I much fear that with such local powers as small boroughs now have, the nuisance cannot be put down but whatever directions the Government may please to give to me . . . shall be cheerfully and promptly attended to.

The Home Office was not impressed by these arguments and told the Mayor that if the civil authorities could not maintain order then the assistance of the military should be requested 'as such a forcible defiance of the law year after year ought no longer to have been permitted'. The authorities deserved criticism for their apathy but the solution to the town's problem was not simple. The disturbances could not be put down by force alone. The complexity of the problem was discussed that year by an inquest jury looking into the tragic death of a boy killed by fireworks.

The boy was the son of a bricklayer and shopkeeper in Stoke who had been letting off fireworks in the garden when the sparks from one caused others in his pockets to explode. The inquest chaired by the Borough Coroner at the Sawyers Arms in Stoke declared a verdict of accidental death but the incident caused the inquest jury to reflect on the Guy Riots. The Coroner reminded everyone that there were accidents every year and each year the disturbances became worse. He was sorry to say that too many people in respectable positions were found to approve of behaviour which was both wicked and illegal. Some, he said, did so for amusement and some, though he considered them to be only a few, for political reasons. The discussion ended with a resolution condemning the riots: 'The jury desire to state their unanimous opinion that the dangerous practice of kindling bonfires and letting off fireworks on every Fifth of November in the borough ought to be put down; and they therefore call upon the public authorities to suppress such illegal proceedings; and the jurors will give their individual aid to the authorities for this purpose'.

But what could be done? What weapons did the authorities have? These matters were also discussed by the Coroner and the

Family enjoying Bonfire Night

jury. The main force of law and order in the town was the police
force but this was very small. 'At the moment the magistrates of
the borough can do nothing', the Coroner said, 'They can't go
and seize 100 men disguised with blackened faces or otherwise.
The only force at their command is three policemen, and taken
from the 76 allowed to the county it is a fair proportion'.

One juror recommended swearing in citizens as special constables
but the Coroner considered them to be useless. He had been sworn
in twice. On one occasion he tumbled into a kennel. On another
only two men turned up at the Town Hall out of the thirty-six
who had been sworn in. Only eight could be mustered after
repeated efforts. The Coroner also had no faith in public meetings.
Meetings had been held over and over again, he said. On one
occasion Mr Lee, the then High Bailiff, had nearly all the clothes
torn from his back for the part he played at a meeting. Unless the
inhabitants co-operated with the magistracy the Coroner could see
no way of stopping the demonstrations.

'We want', he said, 'the impulse of a cojoint action between the inhabitants and the authorities'. He also thought that new legislation was needed to cover damage to property. Under the existing legislation damage to houses was paid out of the highways rates from all the parishes in the hundred. This law did not however, cover palings. If it did then all the rate-payers would have an interest in stopping the disturbances.

So the town was not very well equipped for tackling the Guys but the Home Office had said that the riots must be stopped and the authorities decided they should obey. Over the next few years the forces of law and order in the town were severely tested. If we are to appreciate their efforts and and understand their failures we must first look at how they operated. We start with the Guildford Police Force.

THE GUILDFORD POLICE FORCE

In 1832 there were two constables, five tithingmen and two night watchmen who were also sworn in as constables. The constables and their assistants (the tithingmen) were appointed by the town authorities and were positions that dated back to the Middle Ages. Their job was to enforce the decisions of the town authorities, whether they be helping to run the Poor Law, collecting rates or apprehending criminals. The night watchmen were appointed under a local act obtained by the Town Corporation in 1759 to set up a separate board of trustees. These trustees were empowered to levy a rate and appointed watchmen to patrol the town at night. Some instructions, dated 1760, decreed that the watchmen had to patrol every hour from the Town Hall from eleven at night to five the following morning crying out the hour and the weather loudly and frequently 'which will inform every person as hears that the watchmen are doing their duty'. John Mason remembered the situation before 1835:

Previous to the introduction of the police, the old watch being on duty only at night, the maintenance of order fell to the lot of the parish constable, who was appointed by the vestry, and were summoned to quell disturbances. They also did the duty of relieving officers.

The property and person of the inhabitants of the town was protected by three night watchmen, Wilkins being, I think, the oldest. They started their rounds in winter at 8 o'clock carrying lanterns, and called during the night the hour and the state of the weather, especially when near the houses of the aristocracy.

Under this state of things the boys enjoyed a happy state of freedom. They had no fear of 'Bobby' before their eyes.

Corn Exchange, Guildford

In 1835 the Municipal Corporations Act changed the system of law enforcement all over the country. Following the success of the Metropolitan Police (founded in 1829) the Act forced every town to set up a paid body of police to maintain peace in the area. The Act, however, gave the town authorities plenty of scope in deciding what sort of force they established. The Guildford Watch Committee dutifully held its first meeting in January 1836 and appointed three watching and night constables, four constables, a watchhouse keeper and a superintendent. There were presumably teething problems because the four constables who were paid £5 a year were soon replaced by two day policemen. Although there were two less law officers the higher salary bill represented an increase in the town's commitment to its police. In 1841, however, when the passing of the Act was probably considered safely in the past the town cut its force down to three men called: watchmen and policemen plus a superintendent. It stayed at this figure until 1851, when the Guildford Police were amalgamated with the county police force. The number of policemen allocated to the town remained, however, at four.

So much for the history of the force up to 1852. Where were they based and what did they do? By the mid-1840s the police were housed in Tunsgate. In those days the four columns, moved apart this century to permit through traffic, were evenly spaced. Behind them was a 40-foot piazza which served as a cornmarket for most of the year, and was decked out with seats and witness boxes once a year for the county sessions when a travelling judge came to try cases beyond the powers of the borough courts. At the back of this square were some public offices, including the police station, a residence for the superintendent of the police and cages for male and female delinquents.

The minutes of the Watch Committee recorded the provisioning of the police. Six pairs of handcuffs were ordered for the constable in 1836 and a bushel of coal was provided each week in the winter for fires. The Committee followed other towns by clothing the policemen in the same way as the Metropolitan Police, whose uniforms mirrored the fashion of the day. Top hats and frock coats were worn to give the impression that the police were a civilian force serving the community and not a military force threatening it. In 1843 it was decided that the Guildford Policemen would be allocated two pairs of shoes a year. Local tailors were invited to put in tenders for the uniforms. These consisted of a frock coat, two pairs of trousers, one hat, one pair of shoes, a greatcoat and a waterproof cape.

The duties of the police were summarised in 1851 as attending all public meetings in the borough, all council and committee meetings and sittings of the County Court. Odd references in the local newspapers for 1850 provide extra detail. Policemen's duties varied from attending local cricket matches on pleasant afternoons to patrolling the streets alone all hours of the night. Drunken agricultural labourers found lying asleep in the street were regularly taken to the police station to dry out. Public houses were watched in case they continued serving after 11pm (and many tried to); loiterers and vagrants were challenged and moved on. There were examples of police heavy-handedness such as the occasion when P.C. Lewis found two men loitering late at night. After an abusive exchange of words, Lewis tried to hit one of the men but was himself knocked to the ground by the other. One of the men escaped but Lewis dragged the other back to the police station. The Superintendent scented this was just an argument when he saw Lewis arrive. He leaned out of the window and told Lewis to let the man go and return to duty. More serious was the murder of a curate in Frimley who was shot as he struggled with some burglars. The police picked up three suspects and housed them in the police cells until they were taken to court. An excited crowd gathered in Guildford High Street to watch the suspects cross the road for their hearing in the Town Hall.

The colourful descriptions in the newspapers fail, however, to show what it was like to be a policeman in Guildford. It is important to remember that early police forces were underpaid and overworked. For a detailed look at the duties of the Guildford Police we must go back to the Watch Committee minutes of 1836. One of the policemen was to arrive at the police station' at 6am to receive a report from the night watchman. He then worked until 8.30pm. The other policeman started and finished an hour later. They were allowed breaks for meals but at different times from each other. There was an hour for breakfast and dinner, and half an hour at the end of the day for tea. They had to attend Divine Service on Sundays (one in the morning and one in the afternoon). When these rules were written, there were three watchmen and night constables and two day policemen and a superintendent. By the 1850s there were only four men, including the superintendent, and two of them were night policemen. In 1855 the superintendent complained that he was totally overstretched and if a policeman was sick or injured there was no one to cover.

In these circumstances it is not surprising that the Guildford police force followed the pattern of other police forces in having a high turnover. Curiously, up to 1841, when the force was reduced to three men and a superintendent, there was a small turnover but in the nine years that followed there were frequent changes. The superintendent and one of the policemen remained in post throughout the period, but the other two posts were filled by twelve other men. Five of these men were dismissed for drunkenness or neglect of duty, and eight of them served for less than eighteen months.

A cheap and easy solution to the shortage of police was the use of special constables, and it is to them that we must now turn.

SPECIAL CONSTABLES

Special constables were appointed in accordance with an 1831 Act 'For Amending the Laws Relative to the Appointment of Special Constables and for the Better Preservation of the Peace'. Justices of the Peace who feared that a riot might take place were allowed to appoint as many householders as they desired for as long as necessary. Some householders were exempt from performing this duty but the Secretary of State could remove the exemptions. Justices had power to make rules to regulate the special constables who had the same powers as police constables. If householders failed to carry out their duties they could be fined up to £5.

A fair amount of information exists concerning the operation of special constables in Guildford during the Guy Riots. The numbers appointed varied from year to year from fifty to 400 or 500, depending on the seriousness of the situation. They were enrolled for varying periods, sometimes as long as three months but one 'special' recalled being enrolled for only fourteen days. According to Henry Peak the 'specials', when on duty, were divided into small groups under influential men who were known as 'captains'. In an emergency, the Town Hall bell was rung to summons all 'specials' within earshot. If a riot was anticipated then the 'specials' were posted in certain parts of the town.

The job cannot have been a pleasant one. Henry Peak served as a 'special' and recalled 'the ordeal we had to pass through night after night parading the damp and dismal streets for hours'. Another 'special' recorded parading the town from 5.30pm to 1am on 5th-6th November 1863. On several occasions he was on duty until the small hours of the morning. As well as being unpleasant it must have been a frightening job.

The attitudes of the 'specials' to their duties varied. No doubt quite a few took the job seriously. 'I hope now a final stop is put to these disgraceful proceedings', wrote a volunteer in December 1865. Some were over enthusiastic. John Mason recalled how one Goliath-size burgess turned out one night with a crowbar. In a letter dated 7th November 1855, a visitor to the town complained of being roughly treated. He arrived by train at 8.30pm and walked across the bridge to the High Street, where he was 'set upon by two ill-mannerly ruffians, who forcibly detained me and took a small parcel from under my arm, inquiring at the time who I was and my business'. His first impulse was to use his fists, but on consideration he asked for an explanation and was told that his assailants were special constables and that the magistrates had told them to interrogate all men of a suspicious character.

Plenty of 'specials' were the opposite extreme. As the Borough Coroner recalled, many were reluctant to carry out their duties. In 1853 ten 'specials' were fined for not turning up. In 1856 a Mr Chennel was summoned before the magistrates for failing to turn up when summoned on 13th October. He said he had performed the duties of a special constable before and there were others on the list who had not; he did not see why he should do the job. Those who did turn up did not always stay throughout the night. John Mason was one of a body of twelve 'specials' stationed at Tunsgate who should have remained there until three the following morning. One by one, however, they disappeared and when a roll call was taken the following morning only a few remained.

METROPOLITAN POLICE, COUNTY POLICE AND ARMY

The 'specials' were thus a mixed bunch and, as will be seen, they were not very effective against the Guys. In the years that followed the establishment of local forces, magistrates frequently turned to the Metropolitan Police for assistance at public gatherings. In 1838 Guildford asked for a Metropolitan policeman to be sent to the town for the winter. The Metropolitan Police refused but did send two policemen to the town for a fair on 22nd November. This reliance on the Metropolitan Police was one of the reasons why the County Police Act was passed in 1839 allowing counties to set up their own forces. After 1851 a county police force existed in Surrey and in theory it could be used to supplement the Guildford police. The county police force, however, was formed to police the rural areas and was not usually available for use in Guildford on 5th November.

Metropolitan Policemen

Finally there was the army. Troops had not been used in Guildford since 1805, when four dragoons were called out by the Chief Magistrate, Mr Harrison, to tackle a riot. Some people, however, complained of sword cuts and the officer in command was court marshalled for obeying Harrison's instructions. Soldiers were trained to kill and using them on civilians remained unpopular.

LEGAL MEASURES

As well as these different forces there were also various laws. There was a £5 fine under a local paving Act for selling fireworks and a 40-shilling fine for letting them off in the borough. The Highway Act said that no fireworks should be let off, even in gardens, within a certain distance of the highway. It was, however, very difficult to punish offenders effectively. Often there was not enough evidence to prosecute. The offences that were brought before the magistrates, such as letting off fireworks, stealing fences, lighting bonfires and assaulting policemen, were committed in the confusion of a riot on a dark night and the rioters were often disguised. It was therefore easy for a defendant to claim mistaken identity. The police were so stretched that often only one policeman saw the defendant commit the crime and so it was his word against that of the defendant.

Consequently out of a sample of twenty-six men charged during the period of the Guy Riots, whose cases were reported in the local newspapers, eight were dismissed. It is not known why two were discharged. Two others were released in 1843 with a warning while three in 1851 and one in 1855 were let off because there was insufficient evidence to prosecute. Five of the twenty-six received light fines. Two of these would have received heavy fines had more evidence been available. There was also insufficient evidence for the conviction of a man who received a heavy fine in 1856 but as he had a criminal record he was not given the benefit of the doubt. Nine others received heavy fines and the results of the trial for the last two are not known.

When men were given heavy fines the punishment was not always very effective. In 1843 two men were sentenced to gaol when they refused to pay their £3 fines. Their supporters, however, raised the money and paraded the men round the town, smashing the windows of the Police Inspector and the Mayor. In 1847 the outcome for another man who was fined heavily was virtually identical.

One very important piece of legislation was the Riot Act (1715) which permitted very harsh punishments. It stated that a riotous group of twelve or more who failed to disperse within an hour of being ordered to would be regarded as felons. It was a crime to oppose the reading of the Act and anyone who failed to disperse could be arrested. Those trying to disperse a crowd were justified in wounding, and even killing anyone who resisted. Not surprisingly, the Act was a very effective means of dispersing crowds.

CHAPTER V

BATTLE COMMENCES
1853-1857

AS autumn 1853 approached so did the threat of the Guys, but this year the authorities planned to stop the trouble. On 25th October the Town Clerk wrote to the Home Office to explain the plans and to ask for help:

> The magistrates are unwilling to have recourse to the military unless the riot extends to such a pitch as to render it imperatively necessary . . . and it is obvious that unless the military are brought into the town on the day previous to the night of the anticipated riot they could not be brought from their station in time to be available to quell or check the disturbance.

The Surrey Constabulary was not able to provide extra police, so the authorities proposed to swear in 300 special constables. These volunteers needed to be properly led and so the assistance of fifty Metropolitan policemen was requested. The town agreed to pay for them but in the event only ten Metropolitan policemen were sent. The public were made aware of these plans in a proclamation published in the *Sussex Advertiser* on 25th October:

> The Mayor and Magistrates having been legally called upon to exercise their authority for preserving the peace of the borough on the Fifth of November next, hereby give notice, that they will meet in the Council Chamber of the Town Hall and on Wednesday evening next, the 26th October, at half past six o'clock for

the purpose of recording the names of all persons who may
volunteer to be special constables, with the view of rendering
their assistance in preventing a repetition of the unlawful proceedings which for some years past (on that night) have been a
disgrace to the borough. At this meeting the Mayor and Magistrates will nominate and appoint such additional special constables
as they may think necessary for the protection of the inhabitants,
and the security of the property in the borough.

The Mayor and Magistrates have every confidence in the
loyalty and good feeling of their fellow townsmen, and do not

doubt having their support in suppressing any disturbance, should such unhappily take place and they trust that all heads of families and employers will use their best authority for preventing their families and servants being abroad on that night.

The Mayor and Magistrates are desirous that it should be publicly known, that if any person is convicted of the following offences they will be subject themselves to the penalties attached to them.

All persons appearing in Public Highways masked and disguised for an unlawful purpose will be subject themselves to punishment under the Vagrant Act, and render themselves liable to three months imprisonment with hard labour.

If a number of persons assemble together and are riotous and disorderly, they are liable to be indicted and punished by fine and imprisonment.

And should the Mayor and Magistrates think it necessary to read the Riot Act, the persons afterward offending are liable to transportation.

All persons standing and looking on, in the event of a riot, without rendering assistance to the authorities are liable to punishment.

Any persons making a fire or letting off fireworks in the public streets are liable to a fine of five pounds, and in default of payment thereof to imprisonment.

By order of the Mayor and Magistrates
W. Haydon Smallpiece (Clerk)

Three days later another notice was issued:

The Mayor and Magistrates of Guildford recommend gentlemen, heads of family, and others residing in the county, to request all persons over whom they have any influence, not to remain in

The High Street & New Church of St Nicholas, Guildford

Guildford after seven o'clock in the evening on the Fifth of November next.

By order of the Mayor and Magistrates

W. Haydon Smallpiece (Clerk) 28th of October 1853

Bonfire Night came and on 8th November the *Sussex Advertiser* announced, 'The Fifth of November has passed! The night on which generally in this borough the greatest uproar and disorder prevailed has passed, we are happy to say, unaccompanied by any of those violent proceedings by which it has formerly been characterised'. On the previous day the Town Clerk had written proudly to the Home Office announcing that 'perfect order was maintained'.

This was not, however, the end. It was in fact just the beginning. The authorities had fired some warning shots, but the Guys were not going to be deterred easily, and the town could not continually rely on help from the Metropolitan Police. A Home Office official wrote, 'Next year they must rely upon their own resources — this system of lending the Metropolitan Police is very bad in my opinion'. So when 5th November came round again (1854) the defence of the town was left to the local police and special constables, and this time the Guys were ready to tackle the opposition. The Fifth itself passed quietly but on the following night the Guys came out in force. The police and 'specials' failed completely to disperse the mob which divided into groups and marched round the town, smashing windows. Between 9pm and 10pm the mob assembled outside the White Lion Inn which housed the Mayor and magistrates. Only when the Riot Act was read did the crowd go away.

Curiously Bonfire Night passed quietly in 1855, but in 1856 the battle between the mob and the police resumed. The Guys planned their invasion of the town carefully and lured the police into a trap. Soon after 8.30pm the Guys arrived and lit a bonfire outside Holy Trinity. Palings were thrown onto it but the police turned up with some special constables and extinguished the fire. The Guys lit another bonfire on Star Corner (the junction of Quarry Street and High Street). Once again the police put it out. A third bonfire was lit on the bridge and this time the Guys fought back when the police intervened. Stones flew through the air at the police but the battle was short. The efforts of the police were proving useless. Instead of decisively defeating the Guys they had antagonised them and 5th November became a night for fighting. Sooner or later a disaster was bound to happen. It happened the following year.

*   *   *   *

At 9pm on 5th November 1857 the police charged. About three dozen policemen ran down Mount Street towards the bonfire outside St Nicholas Church. In front of the fire stood the Guys and their supporters ready and armed. The police charged into a hail of flints and stones and a policeman fell to the ground, his eye driven out of its socket by a stone. The charge continued. Policemen lashed out with their staves, indiscriminately knocking people to the ground. For a moment the crowd dispersed as the police ran onto the bridge but then it reassembled for a fight. Vicious skirmishes followed. The police charged the mob. The mob charged the police. Both sides seemed determined to smash each others skulls. Old men and children fell victim to staves and stones. Two men had their heads broken by missiles. A sixty-year-old man was knocked to the ground by a policeman as he came to remove his children from the scene. A man with a child in his arms was also hit. Another returning from work was caught up in the fight and received a blow in the mouth from a stave.

The Mayor arrived on the scene and tried to calm the fray by addressing the crowd from the bridge. The bonfire was nearly out so he suggested that they should disperse. The crowd listened and gave three cheers to the Mayor but in the confusion the police charged again. Once again the Mayor intervened and the police retreated pursued by the mob and a hail of stones. Up the High Street the police ran, down Market Street and North Street to the newly built County police station in the Woodbridge Road where the mob contented themselves with smashing windows. They then returned to St Nicholas to fuel their bonfire and eventually dispersed in the small hours of the morning.

The evening had started with a bad omen. A servant girl looking out from the Bull's Head was seriously injured when a firework smashed through the window and exploded. But worse was to come. Around nine o'clock a crowd of between fifty and a hundred people emerged from Mount Street with faggots which they piled up outside St Nicholas Church and ignited. The police on duty tried to intervene but were assailed by flints and large stones. Two constables were knocked to the ground and they went for help. The Mayor and magistrates had anticipated trouble and applied to Captain Hastings, the Chief Constable of the County Constabulary, for some county policemen. Between thirty and forty were sworn in and were patrolling the town under Superintendent Parr

when they heard about the trouble outside St Nicholas Church. Superintendent Parr led his men down Quarry Street, over the river, though Mill Lane, Buryfields and the Portsmouth Road to Mount Street, where the charge began.

There were many injuries but no deaths on the night of the charge. On the following day, however, one of the injured, who had lost a lot of blood from head wounds, was working up a ladder and fell. He later died. To the undoubted relief of the police an inquest returned a verdict of accidental death and did not link the tragedy with the riot. In his report on the charge the Chief Constable tried to deflect criticism from his force by drawing attention to the vicious character of the mob. The mob, the report said, had pulled down gates and palings for its bonfire. Members of the crowd had been disguised with helmets and armed with bludgeons and had assailed the police with stones. Two policemen had been seriously wounded and eight injured. Two court actions against the police had proved unsuccessful. The Chief Constable also shifted any blame away from himself by referring to an Act of Parliament which compelled him to supply police to a borough if the magistrates placed a request. He also reported that the Mayor of Guildford had actually stated in a letter that the police were not to blame.

'Great Ajax!' exclaimed the *West Surrey Times* on 16th January 1858, expressing the view that the report had all the hallmarks of a cover up. 'Does the Police Committee suppose that there is sufficient simplicity in the County of Surrey to enable its enlightened citizens to swallow their report whole and not be troubled with indigestion?' One of the two court cases that the Chief Constable claimed were unsuccessful had failed on technical grounds and the other was not even to do with Guildford but concerned an event in Woking. The Mayor may well have publicly removed the blame from the police but privately the town authorities pointed the finger. In early December, when the bill for the services of the county police came before the Town Council, one of the councillors suggested it should not be paid. The county police he claimed, had 'caused a great deal of trouble, and were promoters of the riot from beginning to end and we were indebted to them for one of the most monstrous outrages which had been committed in our town for a great number of years'.

The *West Surrey Times* was highly critical of the whole episode but gave a very balanced explanation for the likely causes of the tragedy:

> The practice of letting off fireworks in the public street is, doubtless, highly reprehensible but still it is no excuse for acts of violence committed by those whose duty it is to secure order and peace. The remonstrance which the Mayor directed to the Superintendent of Police [during the riot] is sufficient to justify the belief that there was, unfortunately an excess of instructions, if not duty, somewhere.

Clearly the county police were directly to blame for the battle but trouble had been brewing for several years. The conflict was a consequence of the authorities' failure to find a solution to the problem of the Guys and those who put the police in a position where such a riot could take place also deserved criticism. Anyone who had witnessed the battles of the previous four years would have anticipated a serious confrontation sooner or later.

The riot of 1857 was a complete defeat for the forces of law and order on 5th November. The following year it was decided to leave the town to the mercy of the Guys and to hope for the best. Surprisingly the *West Surrey Times* records no reprisals against the police after Bonfire Night. The Guys disappeared to return to their livelihoods until next year.

Seven years had passed since Henry Peak had come to the town. He had seen boisterous celebrations on 5th November turn into warfare. What sort of town had Guildford turned into? Was law and order breaking down? It is worth pausing to look at Guildford in 1858.

CHAPTER VI

GUILDFORD IN 1858

WITH the opening of the year 1858', wrote Henry Peak, 'I may be said to have fairly commenced practice for myself as an Architect and Surveyor'. 1858 was an important year for Henry Peak. He was now twenty-six and had been working for Mr Moss, a local builder, ever since he came to Guildford. Peak was very loyal to Moss but the business was not very successful and for the first couple of years he had to work twelve or thirteen hours a day for no extra pay. The building industry suffered during the Crimean War (1854–6) and at this inopportune moment Moss bought some land in Ash and built on it. Not surprisingly he was unsuccessful in making money out of the venture. He became worried and frequently could not afford to pay Peak's wages. Peak still had plenty of work to do in office hours but the decrease in business gave him free evenings which he put to good use. He supplemented his income by producing drawings for other builders and soon became glad of the contacts. Moss became ill and for some time was unable to work and consequently the business started to go downhill. Peak claimed he would have stayed with Moss if it had been possible but the shortage of work forced him to look elsewhere. He placed an advertisement in the *West Surrey Times* and set up on his own.

Peak's decision to leave Moss was no doubt influenced by his personal situation. When he first arrived in Guildford, Mrs Moss had helped him find lodgings with a Mrs Nye in Commercial Road. Initially Peak worked hard to further his career and when not at the office he studied in his room. After a couple of years he became attracted to Mrs Nye's devoted niece, Miss Dalman, who lived in the house and ran a school there. Her parents had died when she was young and so her aunt had adopted her. The young couple started courting and were eventually married in London on 17th June 1856. Work commitments prevented a honeymoon and they returned to Guildford the same day to a small house in Stoke Fields. Mrs Nye came to live with them and Peak's wife gave up her teaching to help him in his work.

There had been great changes in Peak's life but what about the town he lived in? In spite of its gradual growth, Guildford had not changed much since 1851. It was still a busy market town, with animals filling the High Street every week. Dust still blew into people's houses, and one female resident in the High Street refused to leave home on market days after being jeered at by drovers and nearly knocked down by the animals. The area around the town was still predominantly agricultural and land was still farmed using traditional methods. A fine spring in 1858 showed promise of a good harvest, but by July when labourers took to the fields with their sickles the situation had changed. Hot weather in June ruined some crops whilst strong winds and rain in July uprooted trees and blew off the fruit on others.

Although 5th November had become associated with ferocious battles the *West Surrey Times* gives no indication of trouble at other times. The year was full of traditional events and celebrations that remained peaceful. At Christmas there was the usual carol singing and Morris dancing. The churches were decorated with evergreens and flowers and some gentlemen gave presents to their employees. At the workhouse inmates were given roast beef and plum pudding; the children there were given sweetmeats and oranges and sang carols in the evening. The railway was helping to bring distant relatives within reach, and special trains on Christmas Eve, Christmas Day and Boxing Day enabled families to visit each

HENRY PEAK,

ARCHITECT & SURVEYOR,

GUILDFORD.

HENRY PEAK begs most respectfully to inform those requiring the assistance of a Surveyor, that he is ready to furnish the necessary

DRAWINGS, SPECIFICATIONS, & ESTIMATES,

and to arrange and superintend the erection of every description of building.

Builders, Bricklayers, Carpenters, and others engaged in building operations, furnished with Sketch Plans, Working Drawings, Specifications, &c., and works already executed, measured, and valued on moderate terms.

OFFICE; No. 4. COMMERCIAL ROAD, GUILDFORD.

other. The theatre opened for a short Christmas season with a seasonal entertainment called 'The Honeymoon' and a farce, called 'High Life below Stairs'.

Easter also brought its store of traditions. Shops closed and Church services were held on Good Friday. A cricket match was played on the Prince of Wales cricket ground in Woodbridge Road even though it was snowing and raining. Other people amused themselves by shooting caged rats. On 1st April (All Fools Day) tradesmen and residents received hoax letters and invitations, and several people spent the day on false errands. In May there was a sheep, cattle and horse fair, and at Whitsun the railway put on special trips to the Crystal Palace which had been transferred from Hyde Park to Sydenham. Autumn brought St Catherine's Fair which, although less busy than in the past, still had its colourful assemblage of dancing booths, gingerbread stalls and panoramic peep-shows amongst other stalls.

As in 1851 efforts were being made to tackle the many inadequate services in the town for there was still plenty for Guildfordians to moan about. One problem was the price of water. A public meeting was held in November 1857 to discuss a recent increase in water charges made by the privately owned water company. Considering the importance of the matter ,it was surprising that only twenty people turned up. The views expressed mirrored the meeting held in 1851 about the charges for gas. On behalf of the meeting a Mr King wrote to the Mayor:

> Dear Sir,
>
> At a meeting of the inhabitants held at the Council Chamber to consider the increased rates charged by the proprietors of the Water Works under the Bill lately obtained it was the unanimous opinion of those present that it would be a great advantage to the town generally, if the Town Council could obtain the management of the works, either by purchase at a fair price, or at a rent charge for the shares now held by private individuals.
>
> I am, Sir, your obedient servant
> W. King, Chairman
> 9 December 1857

The letter was discussed at the the next meeting of the Town Council. Mr Sells spoke for half an hour and sent several councillors to sleep with his proposal that they should investigate the possibility of buying the water works. His motion was nevertheless carried.

Mr Sells was a keen campaigner for improvements in the town and he also turned his attention to the fire brigade. As in 1851, only the seriousness of its work prevented it from the being the joke of the town. In November 1857 a fire broke out at a timber yard between the town bridge and the railway station on a site previously used as the gasworks. The fire engines were quickly on the scene and a large crowd helped fight the fire. The timber yard was destroyed but the fire was prevented from spreading to Messrs F. & A. Crooke's brewery next door. There were fears that the gunpowder in the magazine of the militia stores on the opposite side of the river might ignite so water was poured on them. A barge laden with gunpowder was discovered and moved out of harm's way. Further fears came from the royal military train

Guildford from St Catherine's Hill

stationed in the town for the night with guns and horses on its
way to Christchurch, but the fire was fortunately brought under
control. At first sight it would appear that the fire was tackled
successfully but Mr Sells again saw cause to voice concern at the
meeting of the Town Council. The fire broke out near the river
but the fire engines were unable to use the river water. Firstly
their pipes were not long enough to reach the river and secondly
the engines had no suction pipe to draw up the water. To make
matters worse, the three fire engines were stored in different parts
of the town. Fortunately the fire at the timber yard was brought
under control, but Mr Sells's complaint was that the fire service
was inadequate for a town with 10,000 inhabitants.

A fire in April helped prove his point. Fire broke out at Orange
Grove Farm, about two miles from Guildford, and two horses died
as the stable burnt. Neighbours and labourers came out to help

save the granary by drenching it with water, but there was danger of the fire spreading to the farmhouse. Help was immediately sought from the Guildford fire brigade and a rather disorganised group of firemen journeyed to the scene. On turning into the lane from the turnpike road one of the lamps was extinguished and consequently the driver could not see his way along the sandy road. The engine became embedded in a ditch so the horses were given an extra lash to pull it out, but the traces of the harnesses snapped. As a result the engine had to be dragged manually to the fire, arriving after the farmhouse had been saved. This sort of incident only helped Alderman Sell's argument that a properly organised fire brigade was needed. In the autumn the General Purposes Committee was instructed to look into the matter.

As in 1851, we can rely on the workhouse to show us the grim side of the town. Amongst the many people who fell victim to to the 1834 Poor Law were those in search of work. They were not to be given poor relief and therefore until they found work they could not eat and also ran the risk of being arrested and imprisoned for vagrancy which was illegal. This problem came to the attention of the *West Surrey Times* on 8th May 1858 when Mr Ames, the Master of the Guildford Workhouse, took pity on some vagrants and admitted ten over night. This did not go down well with the Board of Guardians, and he had to attend one of their meetings to answer for his actions. The scene could have come directly from a novel by Charles Dickens:

Chairman: I presume you gave them no food?

Mr Ames: I gave a breakfast to four of them who worked for it . . . .We are compelled to do so according to the book of instructions issued by the Board of Guardians.

Clerk: The law says you may do so but it does not say that you shall.

Chairman: I think you have been acting altogether in opposition to the resolution of the Board [of Guardians].

Mr Ames: They told me they had had no food all day.

Chairman: That does not signify . . . .There is a distinct resolution that no food is to be supplied except in those very urgent cases, and you have failed to show that these were urgent cases.

Mr Evershed: The resolution was that Mr Ames should be judge in urgent cases; we never contemplated the relieving officers sending any vagrants.

The Clerk: If they are sent on order Mr Ames must receive them, and when you get them here the fair supposition is that they are cases of necessity and therefore Mr Ames cannot help giving them food.

Chairman: The resolution of the Board says they are to have no food.

Vice-Chairman: I have always seen this difficulty. If vagrants are sent here by the Relieving Officer we must consider them destitute, and the Master is bound to relieve them.

Mr Evershed: The difficulty can easily be surmounted by prohibiting the relieving officer from sending them here.

Mr Harper, the Relieving Officer, was called in.

Chairman: The Board understand that you sent something like ten vagrants here contrary to the resolution of the Board.

Mr Harper:	I could not help it. They had no visible means of subsistence at all. There was only one halfpenny among the whole ten.
Chairman:	Destitution does constitute an urgent case . . . . Do you think that any real injury to the party would result from a refusal of relief?
Mr Harper:	They told me they had had no food all day, and they had no money to get a lodging with.
Chairman:	That does not signify. An able- bodied man would meet with no possible injury by lying in the open air for a night. I find they are nearly all youths — lads. The oldest of them is only forty-three.
Mr Harper:	Then what am I to do when they apply for a lodging?
Major Onslow:	Why, tell them that there is no lodging for them.
Mr Harper:	But, then, suppose anything happens to them.
Chairman:	That I conceive is a question for the Board. We take the responsibility.

Mr Ellis thought that the police should look out for vagrants and pick them up before they applied to the Relieving Officer. Mr Harper, however, pointed out that the police did not like picking them up because of the expense it put on the borough.

Chairman:	Then, Mr Harper, you must be very firm with these men. Of course it is not the intention of the Board to refuse any really urgent case but you must use great caution.
Mr Harper:	Then if a man has no visible means of existence?

Chairman: That is not an urgent case.

Mr Harper: I do not know what an urgent case is.

The Chairman explained that if anyone fainted by the way or was unable to go further then that was an urgent case. It is reassuring to discover that many Guildfordians were as startled by this stern attitude as modern Guildfordians would be. 'I understand that you Guardians have come to a pretty resolution now, and that you are going to let poor people die in the roadside', the Mayor said to one of the members of the Board of Guardians. The *West Surrey Times* looked into the matter and found no justification for the policy. In an editorial the newspaper declared:

> Having heard a great deal about the saving which was to be effected by discontinuing the admission of casual vagrants to the house we became curious to know the sum expended for their maintenance during the last seven years and we have at length discovered that it does not exceed £72. So human beings are to be hunted from place to place like vermin to be imprisoned because they have no money in their pockets, or die by the roadside because they are not imprisoned, and in the latter case Poor Law officials are to run the risk of being hauled up for manslaughter, and all for the saving of £10 a year — a sum which might be covered by making a farthing rate once in nine years . . . .Truly, that body must be composed of excruciatingly economical members.

A letter also appeared in the *West Surrey Times* on the matter on 22nd May.

> Gentlemen — For the last two or three weeks the walls about this town have exhibited a printed placard by which notice is given to vagrants and mendicants that from and after the 24th of April the Guardians of the Union will not allow any orders to any vagrant or mendicants, and that the Master of the Workhouse has instructions to refuse admission to all such persons. Conceiving it to be the main purpose of the appointment of Boards of

GUILDFORD.

Guardians that the money collected in the shape of the poor rates should be applied judiciously in relieving necessitous persons I am entirely at a loss to understand the meaning of the notice to which I respectfully call your attention . . . .My door is frequently assailed by mendicants — when I walk out not a day passes that I do not meet some person who begs alms, and a large proportion of the mendicant are men — some disabled by accident or illness, some able-bodied but in want (as they say) of employment. I have thought myself justified hitherto in refusing to give them alms, and recommended them to apply at the Workhouse, for why do I pay heavy poor rates? but if the needy person should now point to the printed notice, what choice is left to him but between starvation and a gaol? I have always understood that vagrancy and mendicity are punishable offences because the law provides relief in cases of need. A man who travelled all day in search of work and found none, if he beg for alms, or if at night without having the means of procuring a lodging, he lay down in a shed or any place for shelter to sleep, renders himself liable to be committed to prison. These cases are commonly occurring here, but if the workhouse is no longer to receive people under such circumstances, what is to become of them? And again I ask why are the poor rates collected? I cannot believe this resolution of the Board of Guardians of the Guildford Union is legal, and I respectfully submit that it deserves the serious attention of the Poor Law Commissioners — I have the honor to be, Gentlemen

Your very obedient servant
J.C. Hudson
Woodbridge Road
1 May 1858

The matter did receive the attention of the Poor Law Commissioners who solved this dispute by recommending that the police should be made relieving officers. The police could then root out the undeserving cases. The Master had to accept anyone who was sent to him so if he refused anyone who was not sent by the police the problem would be solved. The police were in contact with vagrants all the time and would know whether they were deserving cases. Whether or not this worked is not known but the incident is interesting for revealing contemporary attitudes to poverty. No one was questioning the desirability of the Poor Law. It was not right that people should die in the streets but what happened to them in the Workhouse was not being debated here.

The *West Surrey Times* can only offer us a glimpse of Guildford in 1858, but it is interesting that nowhere in its pages other than in November is there any reference to the Guys. It would be expected that such a rebellious group would have appeared at other times but the Guys seem to have been a problem that was confined to November. In 1858, for example, a parliamentary election took place. It was a lively, exciting occasion which brought deep political convictions to the surface. Had the Guy Riots been an expression of social, religious or political feelings, then the Guys would undoubtedly have turned up on Election Day. But they did not.

In 1858 only 560 Guildfordians were eligible to vote. Urban working class males did not get the vote until 1867 and the secret

The back of the Red Lion inn

ballot did not come in until 1872. Nevertheless reform was definitely a possibility and the whole town took an excited interest in Election Day. Those who could not vote tried to persuade or intimidate those who could. The centre of town became a sea of noisy people. Reports on voting were broadcast throughout the day giving the event the atmosphere of a football match.

The election excitement started when the nominations of the two candidates took place at the Town Hall on Friday 22nd October. Mr Evelyn, representing the Tory Party, emerged from the White Hart Hotel (now Sainsbury's) attended by his committee of thirty or forty, including magistrates, professional men and merchant tradesmen all wearing Tory purple and orange rosettes. A very different crowd escorted the Liberal candidate Mr Onslow from the White Lion (now White Lion Walk). The men were of lower social status and instead of rosettes a few had cards stuck in their hats saying 'Onslow For Ever'.

Inside the Town Hall a crowd listened to the speeches of the two candidates. Mr Onslow said that it was thanks to the Liberal Party that whilst revolutions had raged on the Continent England had been free of them. He demanded an extension in the franchise to all men, along with the secret ballot to protect the voter from his landlord, customers and creditors. Church rates should be abolished to bring down taxation; he argued that the Church of England was the smallest but richest Church in the world and did not deserve support for its maintenance. He opposed the billeting of troops on innkeepers; one publican in Guildford had had 4000 men billeted on him in one year. He would reduce the standing army as it encouraged quarrels but would maintain a large navy. He would also advocate shorter parliaments to prevent ambitious men from staying in power without consulting the electorate.

Mr Evelyn had fewer points to make but warned the electorate that reform could decrease Guildford's representation from two MPs to one. The Liberal *West Surrey Times* said his appeal might have won support 'did not a large number of the electors of Guildford already feel that the elective privilege they now enjoy is becoming irksome to them by entailing a large sacrifice of principle and violation of conscience'.

The Election itself was an exciting affair. Bets were laid as to the winner and long before polling started at eight in the morning crowds had assembled at polling booths round the town. The

An Election Scene

Abbot's Hospital booth was virtually besieged. There was a great struggle in the first hour and at nine o'clock the poll figures were Onslow 121 to Evelyn's 89. A large number of paid men went round the town announcing that Onslow was winning. Over the next hour Mr Evelyn's supporters reduced the gap by five votes but by midday the Liberal lead seemed secure. Liberals went round with placards saying 'Go home Evelyn!' The Tories, seeing that Onslow's main support came from Stoke painted placards insinuating that the Stoke agent was influencing the vote: 'To be seen in full work at Abbot's Hospital the Harwood patent screw'. The excitement outside the Town Hall was now intense. Carriages brought up voters through the thick crowds, boardmen yelled hoarse cries, candidates were cheered as they made an appearance. The contest was virtually over. Onslow had 262 votes to Evelyn's 223 but seventy-five votes remained to bé cast. It was at this point that the first disturbance occurred. The Liberal supporters paraded a placard outside the committee room of the White Hart showing Mr Evelyn on the gallows. Evelyn's supporters could not take this and a punch-up ensued with broken placards and black eyes but no serious injuries. It was only stopped by the intervention of Mr Evelyn. Owing to the pugnacious character of the crowd the candidates withdrew their placards. At three o'clock the votes stood at 267 to 238 in favour of the Liberals. Fifty-five votes remained and rumours spread that Evleyn had a reserve of voters who would turn up at any moment. The rumours proved false. Only two more voters arrived and at 4pm the poll books closed and the church bells rang. And so one of the most exciting days of the year came to a close. Tempers and feelings had run high but there was no sign of the Guys. Where were they?

Two weeks later they turned up.

CHAPTER VII

AT THE MERCY OF THE GUYS

1858-1862

ACCORDING to the *West Surrey Times* the riot of 1857 hardly ceased to be a topic of conversation until the following year. In 1858 there were no police to be seen. Hundreds of people came to the High Street amidst the hiss and boom of crackers. The Guys arrived at ten o'clock disguised and armed with heavy bludgeons. Some wore animal horns on their heads, others were in masks representing the heads of donkeys and other hideous and distorted creatures. Two immense bonfires were lit outside Holy Trinity and opposite Friary Street. They were fed with the usual plunder and the rule of the Guys went unchallenged. A fireball was kicked into a butcher's shop as a punishment for refusing to comply with the established rule of closing early.

Strangely enough this abdication of rule to the mob did not fill everyone with alarm. On the following Monday one of the Guys' victims approached the Borough Bench to enquire as to who should pay for the replacement of his wooden fence. He was told that unless he could produce the guilty person along with proof of the person's guilt he would get no help from the court. It was suggested he should build a brick wall instead. Mr Beldham, painter, who had made the enquiry, may have lost his fence but not his sense of humour. To the great amusement of the court he announced that if he built a brick wall he would deny the Guys their fuel for the following year. This curious willingness to tolerate the vandalism on Bonfire Night occurs again and again along with the more predict-

BELDHAM,
99, HIGH STREET,
GUILDFORD.
PLUMBER, PAINTER,
AND
DECORATER.

J. R. BELDHAM respectfully informs the Nobility, Gentry, and Inhabitants, that all Hydraulic Machines, Closets, Baths, &c., are put up by him upon strictly scientific principles, and warranted to act; and all materials used he guarantees of the best manufacture.

J. R. B. having now had a practical experience of a quarter of a century in the trade, and having of late turned his attention to the sanitary condition generally of Houses and Mansions, and the best means of rendering them habitable, he has taken three primary essentials into consideration, viz., *good water supply, good drainage, and good ventilation;* and having a practical knowledge of the water-bearing soils generally, he may be consulted relative thereto, and plans and estimates furnished.

The Painting Business is carried on upon the same basis, and J. R. B. undertakes the whole cleaning, whiting, papering, painting, and decorating in any style; having studied some of the latest works on Harmony of Colours and their application, he trusts he can produce *good taste, good materials,* and *good workmanship,* which the advancing state of the age calls for.

DESIGNS FOR MEDIÆVA DECORATIONS FURNISHED.

GUILDFORD WATER WORKS OFFICE.

able complaints. Between 1859 and 1862 the Guys had the unopposed run of the town on 5th November and *The West Surrey Times* reported their activities in immense detail.

NOVEMBER 11, 1859

> The town itself was entirely shut up to business transactions, as soon as the evening grew dark, every shop being closed and every window (where available) was rendered impregnable by temporary and permanent shutters. As the night advanced the scenes of disorder increased, and this sorrowful fact became too apparent: — namely that all authority had been abandoned, that government and rule had been suspended, and the whole town, with its property and its inhabitants was given over to an unjust, merciless and ignorant mob, who greedily seize upon this occasion as the time to gratify their vulgar and plundering propensities.

The bonfire was lit in its usual place outside Holy Trinity but the evening was accompanied by accidents and some vicious attacks on individuals and property. Many houses had windows smashed as fireworks darted about the street and one house narrowly escaped destruction when a blind caught alight. Fortunately the people responsible for the accident entered the house and extinguished the fire. Other groups were less considerate. An immense serpent was deliberately thrown through the window of Mr Angel, clothier, in the High Street. A brickbat was hurled through a window at the Town Hall. The house of Mr Powell, of the Prince of Wales Inn, was attacked with bricks. Mrs Powell was only just missed by a brick which flew through the window and smashed a brandy bottle and some glasses. A gentleman coming from the railway station met some Guys and was clubbed on the head for refusing to answer personal questions. A young man received similar treatment without offering any provocation. At one o'clock in the morning two policemen were discovered at Tunsgate and attacked. Despite being struck several times they managed to escape uninjured to the police station. The mob followed them and:

challenged the police to come out and fight. This cordial invitation was politely declined on the part of the whole force, the superintendent telling them that unless they were 'after making themselves scarce', he should fire upon them. They then made an infuriated attack on the station breaking the windows and battering the doors with their clubs so as to disfigure them exceedingly. When the siege was at its most violent climax, Mr Vickers fired off a revolver, the mere explosion of which put the assailants to the rout, and the whole herd of heroes bolted pell mell into the street, and did not return again to the scene of action . . . .There are many other incidents which might be mentioned, all of which tend to show that the Fifth of November proceedings in Guildford will not die a natural death, as some seem to think, for last year there was nothing done by the mob of so outrageous a character as this year, and we would ask, what guarantee have we that the evil which has increased in dimensions this year will not be augmented next? Something must be done to stop this periodical tyranny of a piratical mob.

Surrey GUILDFORD **Times,** GAZETTE,
And General Advertiser for Chertsey, Dorking, Epsom, Farnham, Godalming, Kingston, Reigate, Aldershot, &c.

NOVEMBER 10, 1860

So early as five o'clock the shops began to close, and by six, comparatively speaking, the quiet of a Sunday morning prevailed. Between this time and 8 o'clock, a continued stream of people flowed into the High-street, and gradually changed the scene. Fire balls and rockets began to show themselves in various parts; squibs fizzed; serpents sent forth their brilliant lights, and exploded with a boom that bespoke their power, and gave the signal for numerous other displays . . . During this time hundreds of persons — men, women, boys, and girls — from respectable tradesmen to the rag and bobtail of the back slums, thronged the streets . . . [and] . . . kicked about the fire balls in all directions.

Fires were lit in Mount Street, Castle Street and Millmead. Fireworks were deliberately thrown through the windows of the homes of Mr Napper, Mr Austin and Mr Simmond whilst another passed through the window of Mr Wither's drawing room by accident. The Guys arrived in a procession that was both spectacular and sinister:

A burst of cheers announced the arrival of the Guys, and as 45 armed and masked men poured forth their unearthly sounds and rushed into the throng, a peculiar feeling seemed to influence the lookers on. The men were formed in order four abreast, and each carried a bundle of faggots. In the front row all them bore lighted flambeaux, and were disfigured as follows: — 1st a sugar loafed-shaped hat made of tin-foiled paper, a black mask, and white trousers and slop with red stripes. 2nd, a helmet shaped white hat with horns on the top thrown back, red mask, long white beard, brown slop, blue stockings and knee breeches. 3rd, black hat variegated with strips of pointed tin, a black mask covering his head and shoulders, variegated with tufts of wool, black coat, and white trousers tied up at the knees. 4th, a large old straw bonnet with a carrot protruding about 7 inches in front and a woman's frock. Ten other rows of men equally disfigured, followed in line, bearing torches, bludgeons, and faggots, and as they near the church their wild unearthly appearance, their prolonged and hideous moans, the flash of their flambeaux, the brandishing of their truncheons, and their staring glare through the frightful masks, seemed to send a shudder amongst the amazed spectators. The faggots were deposited in front of the church, and the Guys had vanished in less than five minutes; this time the variegated group were followed by hundreds of spectators who swelled their yells and hideous sounds.

The Guys led the crowd up the Merrow Road to the Union Workhouse. They scaled the wall and carried about 200 bundles of faggots back to the High Street, where:

Rockets, serpents, and other fire-works, were in abundance, and the Guys, evidently in high glee, rushed to and fro in the unearthly, demon like, dance, and ever and anon the whole concourse of people joined in the huzzas that burst forth as the motley throng brandished their weapons of destruction. The chief marched round the fire, and giving a signal for more fuel, they immediately fell into line, like a well organised troop of volunteers, and again merged into the dark bye-ways of the town.

The next forage was down Market Street and along Rays Lane to the premises adjoining Northfield House, where they stole a fence and a gate and stripped the yard in front of a barn. Back they came bearing their spoil on their shoulders whilst others brandished their bludgeons defiantly and beat upon the fencing.

On reaching High-street a deafening yell was raised by the Guys, taken up by the mob, and repeated again and again with terrific fury. Now the Guys felt confident that no opposition would be offered, and on reaching the fire they piled it up higher and higher, and rushed to and fro in full glee. The street contained some thousands of people, the church steps, railings, and every available space on either side of the road being taken up. It was an alarming scene. The fire raged with terrific fury: serpents were hurled every moment amongst the spectators, and exploded with repeated booms: excited Guys brandished their cudgels, turned up the burning posts and rails.

Again the bonfire burnt down. This time the procession went down the High Street, stopping at the Red Lion for some beer and along Quarry Street to Castle Arch, where some fencing was found running from Quarry Street to the Bowling Green. When the Guys returned to the bonfire, they decided they needed some refreshment and turned to the crowd for funds:

At this part of the proceedings the Guys rushed into the various parts of the mob, and in threatening language demanded money from the spectators, and with much success. The respectably dressed lookers on seemed afraid lest their heads should come in contact with the truncheons of the Guys, no one dared to refuse, and thus one man, a most hideous-looking being, with a black mask and long hair, calmly placed his truncheon under his arm, and presented his hands, which were nearly running over with silver and copper, for 'more, more', as he groaned through his nose and teeth, shaking his shaggy head at those who seemed to hesitate. The company having been thoroughly canvassed in this way — which occupied nearly an hour — the entire mob of miscreants quietly proceeded to the 'Lion', and infuriated their demon-like passions with a large supply of drink.

The next excursion was in the direction of Stoke Fields. Yelling and beating gates and walls with their weapons, the Guys arrived at Madhouse Lane where they encountered some opposition:

But here for a moment an obstacle appeared; some men had been paid to protect the paling, and they strove hard to keep their trust. At first they offered the Guys money, but it was of no avail, then they attempted to resist one, when they were immediately surrounded and but for the pleadings of the spectators would have been fearfully beaten by the Guys. It was impossible for the men to save the woodwork, for while they were at the mercy of one portion of the Guys, another had

ENLARGEMENT
OF
"THE WEST SURREY TIMES."

THE Proprietors of THE WEST SURREY TIMES are happy in being enabled to state that on and after Saturday, the 1st of January, 1859, their paper will be issued in a

New and Enlarged Form.

The daily increasing demands upon the space of the paper, in consequence of an extended advertising connexion and the frequent calls for lengthened reports of local occurrences, coupled with the request of numerous correspondents, have induced them to take suitable steps to meet these requirements, and they therefore feel a pleasure in announcing their intention on and after the date before-mentioned, of enlarging the journal to the extent of

Six Additional Columns.

The enlargement will take place without any alteration in the price of the paper, the proprietors being actuated by a simple desire to extend to the utmost possible degree its utility, and to make its capabilities fully commensurate with the character of a county journal.

As a further means of increasing the value of " THE WEST SURREY TIMES " to its readers and supporters, the proprietors have arranged for the printing of the paper by means of

Machinery of the most recent & approved kind,

containing all the modern appliances of the art, which will enable them to supply a much larger number of copies than at present, and, as a consequence, to bring the

Local and other News up to a later hour.

The proprietors trust that this effort to improve the character and form of their paper will meet with a corresponding amount of support at the hands of a discriminating public.

broken down all the fencing, put out and smashed the lamp, and were bearing off the spoil. A long and threatening altercation ensued, and the Guys finally agreed not to injure the interfering parties if they thought good to make themselves off, which they did gladly.

On their way back the Guys picked up some scaffolding poles and water tubs in Ray's Lane, and a tar barrel which they lit and kicked around the High Street.

At this stage in the proceedings it was 12 o'clock, and the throng was still as great as at the commencement. Indeed no one seemed desirous of leaving the scene; the cry was, 'more fuel!', 'more fire!' The serpents and rockets seemed nearly exhausted, but the interest and excitement of the mob seemed immense. The Guys returned again and again with their loads until nearly two o'clock, the people gradually separating the while, and unexpectedly they entirely vanished, when the proceedings were brought to a close by the police — 'gallant' guardians — who attached a hose to the water pipes, and played upon the fire and a few spectators, thereby extinguishing the fire *after* it had been forsaken by its originators.

Surrey Times,
GUILDFORD GAZETTE,
And General Advertiser for Chertsey, Dorking, Epsom, Farnham, Godalming, Kingston, Reigate, Aldershot, &c.

NOVEMBER 9, 1861

The accounts in 1859 and 1860 suggest that the situation was getting increasingly out of control but in 1861 the Guys were much more disciplined in their mischief as the newspaper was happy to report:

The police religiously absented themselves from the streets; the special constables recently sworn in were not called upon to act; and although the chief actors in the Fifth of November drama were so completely masked and disguised that recognition would be impossible, quiet and orderly people were perfectly safe from molestation, and not above half-a-dozen windows were broken probably in the whole town. We think that, considering the opportunities at their disposal, this reflects great credit on the 'managers', whilst it proves that we were not wrong in the estimate that we formed of the good humour always to be found in an English crowd. It is not our own remark, it is the proverbial, and is a common matter of observation with intelligent foreigners, who are astonished at the unruffled temper and imperturbable good nature of enormous concourses of people in this country. We understand that the leaders amongst the movement on this occasion had determined to do as little mischief as possible, to wreak no vengeance upon anyone however unpopular, and to discountenance anything approaching to malicious or even wanton mischief. The great difficulty, however, which they seemed to experience was the want of fuel for bonfires, and in their extremity they made raids upon property which would otherwise doubtless have escaped. As a rule, the object appeared to be to seize only on such wooden fencing and railing as was very old and comparatively valueless, and as belonged to persons to whom the loss would be of no pecuniary consequence. In one or two instances, their discrimination has been at fault, and people have suffered losses which they can ill afford to sustain. We shall be happy to learn that in these cases some compensation has been made to the owners.

Soon after five o'clock, most of the tradesmen and private residents in the High-street, closed their establishments. Some few — including Mr. Weale, Messrs. Austen Brothers, Mr Eager, and others — protected their windows by external boarding up the one, and stopping up the other with sacks and wet straw. Not a light was to be seen in many of the front apartments, and altogether the street presented rather a sombre and dismal appearance for so early an hour. Boys and lads thronged the main thoroughfares of the town, and the constant sharp snapping reports of the crackers, mingled with the heavier boom of the serpents, and the flashes of brilliant light which ever and anon darted across the street and caused consternation amongst the little knots into which the missiles were flung, proved that the juveniles had a plentiful store of fireworks at their disposal. As the hour wore on, the street became more thronged, and the reports of explosives louder and more frequent. By seven o'clock, a considerable number of persons had gathered about the lower part of the town, and by degrees they worked their way up to Trinity Church, where they awaited the approach of the great attraction of the evening. By this time also the youthful portion of the community, animated doubtless by the 'true blue Protestant zeal', had kindled a fire in Chapel Street, opposite the Rose and Crown, whilst a smaller band of enthusiasts had ignited one in South Street, opposite the entrance to Trinity Churchyard; and another set had started one at a short distance up the Mount, opposite the Wheatsheaf. But these although they attracted a considerable concourse of spectators, and were so far useful as drawing away a portion of the crowd from the High Street, were only a subsidiary to the great event which came off in front of the steps of Holy Trinity Church. At a few minutes before nine o'clock, that peculiar sound proceeding from the swell of numberless voices, and the cry of 'loo, loo' which rose upon the air, announced the approach of the 'Guys', and away rushed the crowd to meet them. These mysterious beings who 'Come like spirits, so depart' first made their presence known to mortal ken in the Woodbridge Road, and thence proceeding by the Stoke

Road, Chertsey Street, and Ram Corner, four abreast and laden with hurdles, railings, gate posts, and fences, they emerged into the High Street and made straight for the accustomed spot. The Guys appeared to number between 40 and 50, and they were arrayed in every conceivable variety of exaggerated costume. All wore impenetrable masks, and the whole made up a group more nearly resembling the grand army of Bombasters Furioso as represented on the stage that anything that we can readily call to mind. One who appeared to be a kind of leader wore the smart tight-fitting red coat and helmet of a dragoon; the head of another was adorned with horns such as Bruns ascribes to 'Auld Nickle Ben'; others had black crape and hideously painted masks whilst some had nether garments similar to those of the clown in the pantomime; others had round and painted smocks, militia coats; and two or three wore female habiliments, presenting not a bad impersonation of 'Moll Flanders'; whilst all sorts of fantastical contrivances were had recourse to in order to destroy the identity of the wearers with their ordinary selves.

Abbot's Hospital, Guildford

Immediately upon the arrival of the Guys the fire was piled and kindled with amazing rapidity. The night at that period was brilliantly fine. There was no moon; but the stars shone clear and radiant in the heavens; a slight breeze from the north gently fanned the flames, and brought out the fine proportions of Trinity Church in bold and striking relief. It was a strange sight — the Guys in their extraordinary dresses of every conceivable colour dancing round the enormous fire, the multitude of people massed into a dense throng in the churchyard, on the railings, and in the street, upon whose faces the flames shed a light so strong that every feature was clearly distinguishable; and the brilliant coruscations proceeding every instant from some firework or another as darted through the air, leaving for a moment a fiery gleam in its track, and then a darkness even more profound than before.

The fire once lit burned with immense rapidity; its flames shot up to a level with the first floor windows of the surrounding houses and the myriads of sparks which rose in showers illumined the surrounding sky. So rapidly did the fire burn, and the material of which it was composed consume, that it was evident, if it were to be kept alive, that fresh fuel must be found to feed it. The Guys hold a short conference, cross their clubs; the ominous 'loo, loo' again is heard and the away they start surrounded by an immense body of admiring followers.

They went down Stoke Road and took some timber and palings adjoining a barn. At the White Horse in Spital Street they tried to take some wood being used for building. The owner gave them some beer and persuaded them to take some old timber and leave the new. Back at Stoke Road they took a cart laden with wood. The wood was consigned to the flames and the cart would have followed but 'a respectable townsman considerately interfered, and on his suggestion the cart was wheeled back to the Dolphin Inn, Chertsey Street, where it was safely housed, the Guys being liberally rewarded for their compliance by a few gallons of beer'. The fourth journey was along Friary Street, Commercial Road to Madhouse Lane where Mr Mason was building a house for the Reverend Mr Shrubb. In pulling some gates off their hinges, the

Guys knocked down the wall to which the gates were attached. Coming back via Leapale Road they hauled down a board at the corner of North Street advertising the value of the Leapale Estate for development.

Passing at the bottom of the Commercial road, one or two of the party were about to pull up some rotten pales which appeared to be of no great value, when a word was passed amongst the Guys 'poor woman', 'poor woman', and they immediately desisted from their attempts. Several instances of this nature have been reported to us, and we may add that when some of the mob proposed to knock down some eligible palings in front of Mr. R.J. Sheperd's house in the London-road, they were deterred by the cry of 'good man', which was instantly raised by some of the most active of the Guys. The fifth excursion was in the direction of the Rat's Castle in the Merrow Road, where it is stated they had set their minds upon a couple of waggons; but they were dissuaded from this, and satisfied themselves with a small quantity of old wood. They then crossed down the Waterden-road, and returned up the London-road, where they completely stripped off the wooden railings erected on a dwarf brick wall in front of a small house in the occupation of Miss Rance. We believe that this lady was very much alarmed, and this is one of those cases in which, if possible, some restitution ought to be made. They again visited the White Horse, where they brought away some more old timber which they had obtained leave to take, and this we believe was the last of the journeys in search of fuel. It was now about half past eleven o'clock. The fire burned brilliantly, the crackers, squibs, and serpents were perpetually exploding with undiminished vigour, when suddenly the Guys darted off, and were to be seen no more, their disappearance being even more rapid and mysterious than their approach. One or two men disguised, but not apparently belonging to the regular organisation, still lingered on the scene, and made another foray in search of wood. Upon this occasion they visited the houses of Messrs, Wright, Ransome, Tubbs, Harrington, and Mason, in Buryfields, from each of whose premises they abstracted the palings, and any loose timber that was available. But this was the last fitful effort, drops of rain began very shortly afterwards to descend; the stars became obscured; dark masses of beetling clouds rolled athwart the sky, and a torrent of rain commencing to fall which was evidently the prelude of a thoroughly wet night, very soon scattered the few remaining participators in the revels, and almost in less time than it takes to tell the story, the street was cleared of its occupants, and the dying embers of the fire were finally extinguished.

It will be seen from the preceding notice, that the spirit of good humour which we have so strongly urged for the last week or two, was very generally prevalent. There was none of that ferocious brutality exhibited, which is said to have accompanied similar exhibitions in former years. We are not aware that ribald conversation or disgusting language was had recourse to, and so far as we have heard no one experienced any personal ill-treatment at the hands of the mob. In the town itself very little damage was done, and we only regret that in one or two cases palings were stripped from the premises of persons who are probably not very well able to sustain the loss they have suffered. We have already alluded to one such case; and probably persons might have been found to whom the damage would have been of less consequence than it may be to Mr Bristow and Mr Chaplin, of Chertsey Street. Of broken windows we are only able to enumerate one at our own office, one at Mr Butler's, surgeon, Spital Street, one at Mr W. Stevens, High Street, two at the Red Lion Inn, Market Street, and nine of the small panes at Trinity Church — all, we believe, purely accidental.

Amongst the ludicrous incidents connected with the affair, we may mention the explosion of a large packet of squibs and serpents, which took place on the body of the Guy, who wore the dragoon helmet. It appears that this person carried his fireworks exposed in a bag, which was suspended at his back, and that whilst dancing round the fire, they accidentally became ignited. This caused a most terrific explosion, not more to the discomfort of the gallant Guy, than the amusement of the spectators! Another laughable incident was the reception which a number of juvenile Guys met with in the early part of the evening, at Mr W.H. Smallpiece's. They were encountered by the gardener, Mr Baxendine, with a couple of garden engines, which let play upon them so vigourously, that the juveniles started

Holy Trinity Church

off helter-skelter, and a pace which just saved their skins and 'kept their powder dry'. Some amusement was also created by the eccentric gyrations of the serpents, after they had been ignited and thrown amongst a crowd of people; and when a cracker came into unpleasant contiguity with some venturesome female, she was reminded, not less forcibly by the pertinacity with which the tiresome cracker seemed to follow her, than by the laughter at some of her own evolutions that probably the best place for her would have been at home and in bed.

NOVEMBER 8, 1862

By 1862 the format of Bonfire Night was an established tradition and, provided the mischief did not get out of hand there were still those who thought it was essentially a very nice tradition. About the 1862 celebrations the *West Surrey Times* wrote:

> The police were very wisely kept out of sight upon this occasion. Their absence doubtless tended to the good humour which was generally observable; and although one or two acts were committed, which we had rather had been omitted from the programme, we do not see anything in the occurrence of this 5th of November now last past, which need cause any serious regret or any very general desire, that the observance of this Festival should cease to be commemorated.

As early as five o'clock the shops in the High Street and other busy thoroughfares were closed and barricades erected on some. Squibs and crackers made their traditional early evening appearance in the High Street and several bonfires were lit in different parts of the town. At nine o'clock the familiar cry of 'loo, loo' was heard as the torchlit procession of the Guys entered the town via the Portsmouth Road. As in previous years there were about forty Guys in strange costumes carrying cudgels and large quantities of palings for a bonfire. Most of the palings came from Mr Baxendine's House in Buryfields in revenge for his spraying boys the previous year with water from a garden engine. Soon an enormous bonfire was blazing outside Holy Trinity Church; the flames soared into the sky illuminating the brilliant brickwork of the church. The *West Surrey Times* reported, 'The manifest care which was taken whilst hundreds of fireworks were being exploded, to avoid all the windows in the vicinity . . . showed that mischief, for the mere sake, of mischief, formed no part of the present programme'.

The Guys displayed their unusual loyalty by singing 'God Save the Queen' as they danced round the bonfire. Soon more fuel was needed so they set off on several excursions for firewood. At one stage they came to a house that had been occupied for 19 years by a poor man, John Sutcliffe, and his wife. Owing to the disputed ownership of the house the couple had paid no rent, but two years previously Mrs Sutcliffe, by then a widow, had been evicted by a Godalming solicitor. The house had remained tenantless ever since and the Guys demonstrated their feelings on the matter by smashing all its windows and removing all the doors and other timber they could find for their bonfire.

On the other hand the Guys showed leniency to old Mrs Shepperd the lodge keeper of the Woodbridge Estate. They stole palings from the vicinity of her house they preserved the fencing round her lodge. Unfortunately for the Guys not everyone appreciated the 'good humour' and for the first time in several years someone decided to complain to the Home Office.

6th November 1862

Right Honourable Sir,

Last night about ten o'clock I was called to my door by a mob of from 300 to 400 persons many of whom were masked and were otherwise disguised and armed with most formidable bludgeons. The leader shook a tin canister before me and demanded money. I told him I had none for him. He then shook the base more violently and this was accompanied by movement among the mob which told me the most prudent course was to comply with the demand which I did. They then left me without doing any mischief. This system of levying Black Mail has been carried on for some years and must be well known to the Mayor and authorities of the town and no steps whatever have been taken for several years to stop these proceedings.

I have thought it right to acquaint you with these facts and also that the mob were in the uncontrolled possession of the town for about 6 hours doing great damage to property. One unoccupied house was quite gutted, eight fires were burning in various streets of the town all supplied with stolen fences, &c.

I am, right honourable sir, your obedient servant

Mark Dowlen

I must ask as a favour you will not let my name be known to the authorities here or my house will not be safe from attack by the mob.

The Home Office decided to send a copy of this letter to the town authorities asking for a report. Mr Piper, Mayor, replied on 19th November with a letter that was as full of excuses as his predecessor's in 1852.

Sir,

I beg to acknowledge the receipt of your letter of the 12th instant and in reply thereto beg to state that it is quite true as stated by your informant that there was a great mob in the Borough on the evening of the 5th November consisting of 400 to 500 persons, many of them in disguise, and that there were several bonfires lighted and a great number of Fireworks let off in the streets of the Borough on that evening, that an unoccupied House was quite gutted and considerable damage done to the Fences, Paling and Gates of the inhabitants by being pulled down and carried off to supply fuel to these Bonfires — these disturbances take place annually on the 5th of November and the Magistrates have several times attempted to put a stop to them but have failed to do so. The Constabulary Force of the Borough is utterly inadequate to put them down and on former occasions the County Constabulary and members of the Metropolitan Police have been employed to render them aid in putting them down but all these arrangements have failed and then the disturbances could only have been stopped by calling out the Military which would necessarily have led to Bloodshed. The Magistrates have also in former years communicated with the Home Office with respect to the means to be adopted for putting an end to these annual disturbances and I beg to call your attention to a letter dated the 15th December 1859 from the Clerk to the Magistrates of the borough in reply to one received by the Home Office and also to another letter from the same gentleman to the Home Office dated 6th October 1860. These letters will sufficiently show how desirous the Magistrates have been to put an end to the above occurrences referred to and the means they have adopted in furtherance of that object.

I beg also to call your attention to the fact that in the event of any of the persons concerned in the above proceedings being afterwards brought before the magistrates and being charged with either of the following offences viz with letting off fireworks, with lighting fires, or with being disguised in the streets, the only punishment which the magistrates are empowered by the present acts to inflict upon them is a pecuniary fine which is immediately subscribed for the accused and is in fact no punishment at all. And I, in conjunction with my Brother Magistrates beg to suggest that if in the ensuing Session a clause were to be introduced in some act of Parliament making all or any of the above offences punishable with imprisonment at the discretion of the justices for any term not exceeding three calendar months with a severer punishment to a Second Conviction the Magistrates would on next 5th of November take proceedings to have some of the persons concerned detected and summoned before them and would sentence them to a term of imprisonment which I think might possibly tend to prevent a recurrence of these annual disturbances.

The magistrates would feel much obliged to you if you would lend your advice and assistance in putting down this nuisance and would be glad if you could suggest any course that you think might properly be adopted to them for this purpose.

I have the honour to be, sir, your obedient servant,

H. Piper
Mayor

Abbot's Hospital, Guildford

The Home Office was not impressed and could not see why Guildford was different from other towns. The weeks went by and 5th November passed into memory. The participants returned to their normal existence unaware that they had taken part in the last traditional Bonfire Night in Guildford. Any hopes the Guildford authorities might have had of a compromise with the Guys were completely destroyed by two events in 1863. Both were colourful and enjoyable occasions, but both were accompanied by unacceptable behaviour that plunged the town into disgrace.

CHAPTER VIII

A TOWN IN DISGRACE

1863

THE ROYAL WEDDING

A slight mist hung in the air as dawn broke. Gradually the air cleared and the sun cheerfully lit up the neighbourhood, to the relief of those who had been decorating the streets. From the top of Spital Street to the bottom of the High Street flags hung from buildings and across the road, flapping lazily in the gentle breeze. Then at 6am a chorus of church bells woke the town. It was 10th March 1863 — the wedding of the Prince of Wales to Princess Alexandra.

The day was packed with festivities but was marred by the sinister arrival of the Guys in the evening. Nevertheless whilst daylight remained Guildford was full of joy. The main event of the morning was a parade round the town. By 10.30am the streets were lined by thousands of spectators. The procession started off from the White Horse about an hour later. It must have been an impressive spectacle being over half a mile long. At the front were flags and bands of the 2nd Surrey Militia and the 13th Surrey Rifle Volunteers, followed by old people and schoolchildren wearing rosettes and carrying flaglettes and bannerettes. Stoke School carried two crowns and the Prince of Wales's feathers worked in laurel and roses on a wire frame. Bringing up the rear came the band of the Union Workhouse and the 24th Surrey Rifle Volunteers with their band. The procession went down the High Street, over the bridge and up Mount Street where it regrouped and returned over the bridge, along Friary Street to North Street, ending at the Public Halls. The old people fell out for a meal and the children went to the drill shed of the 24th Surrey Rifles for a bun and orange.

Most of the day's celebrations were paid for by public subscription. Nearly 300 old people attended a dinner at the County and Borough Halls. They sat along four rows of tables laid out in the hall. The meal was preceded by the militia band playing 'Roast the Beef of Old England' and a choir which sang 'God Bless the Prince of Wales'. This done the poor folks (who had been asked to supply their own knives and forks) were allowed to tuck into a meal of roast and boiled cold meat, hot potatoes, hot plum pudding and plenty of beer. One hundred other people too sick to attend were each given two shillings (the cost of the meal). At the end of the meal the band played 'God Save the Queen'.

The generosity of the organisers did not, however, stretch to the poor people in the Workhouse. Furthermore the guardians of the workhouse 'with that chilling want of charity which always seems to steal the heart and freeze the sympathies of the guardians, refused to make extra provision' for the poor they looked after. Fortunately a Mr Whitburn managed to raise enough money to pay for the inhabitants of the Workhouse to have a meal similar to that of the other poor.

The afternoon opened at one o'clock with a gun salute from the 24th Surrey Volunteers followed by the playing of the National Anthem. Both adults and children took part in football, foot races, bobbing in tubs for oranges, climbing the greasy pole, sack races and games of 'Kissing-in-the-ring'. In the latter game the *West Surrey Times* observed that several prudish women confined themselves to all female rings or those with children. The younger women, however, were not so inhibited and thoroughly enjoyed the game. The bands of the 24th Surrey Rifles, 2nd Royal Surrey

GUILDFORD PUBLIC HALL.

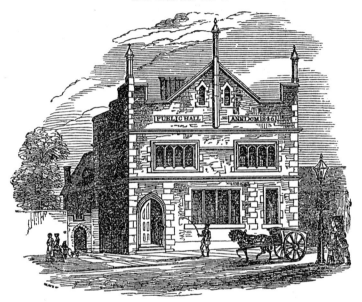

The large or smaller Rooms of this Building are let for the purposes of Societies, Lectures, Concerts, Public Exhibitions or Sales, Balls, Dinners, Tea or other Parties, Religious, Secular, Political, or Committee Meetings, &c.

The Tariff of Charges may be obtained of the Honorary Secretary, Mr. LEMARE, 44, High Street.

Militia and the drums and fifes of the Union Workhouse children made the most of the day and accompanied the proceedings.

At half past four 1700 children were entertained to tea and cake in the drill hall at the Militia Depot. The ancient suits of armour hanging on the walls were brightened up with flags and banners and looked down on the noisy rows of children sitting on long forms. Great barrels of tea were rolled out and amateur waiters went round pouring the beverage into mugs. In spite of the difficulty of serving such large numbers the tea was piping hot. 'Yes, it ort to be blowed, that it ort to', recommended a little girl on scalding her lips. The reporter from the *West Surrey Times* cheekily reported, 'We were in the awful presence of 1700 children — the majority females we should say from the incessant chatter of tongues, which nothing but the immediate supply of tea and cake can stop. We mean no disparagement to the gentler sex by the delicate suggestion: — only a compliment to their superior conversational powers'.

Meanwhile two football matches were being held in the High Street. The players at the bottom of the town were hindered by their proximity to the river and had to retrieve the ball from the water on several occasions. The whole day seemed to be very successful and provided a lot of enjoyment for the whole town. As darkness fell, however, things started to go wrong. A 'Grand Display of Fireworks' was promised in a field adjoining the Farnham Road. There was, however, nothing grand about the presentation. The newspaper reported: 'Roman candles would not ignite; wheels would not revolve, rockets would not ascend; flower pots would not bloom; mines would not explode; crackers would not crack; and serpents refused to perform any of the functions of their tribe beyond hissing — a feat in the accomplishment of which the disappointed spectators readily assisted'. In a fit of frustration quite out of keeping with the spirit of the day the crowd seized the platform on which the fireworks had been displayed and broke it up for a bonfire. The question of a bonfire was another bone of contention. From the Hogs Back it was possible with a night glass to see about 120. From Pewley Hill a further forty or fifty could be spotted. All Surrey seemed to be celebrating the wedding day with bonfires including villages as close as St Martha's where a brilliant fire burned. Guildford, however, had decided to be an exception. The *West Surrey Times* (14th March 1863) takes up the story:

> Undoubtedly the committee who undertook the management of the Guildford Festivities committed a great mistake in not providing for a bonfire, either in the High Street or in some spot of easy access . . . .The consequence was what any sensible man might have expected . . . .It was attempted to make Guildford unlike every other place in the county, by having no bonfire. Well, there exists in this town as most people are aware, a loyal and conservative body who maintain old institutions, and stand by ancient customs: — the throne, the constitution, the Protestant Religion and the bonfire — and who are apt, upon occasions, to repair any little omissions of which our pastors and masters may be guilty. They always show what ardent Protestants and Conservatives they are on the 5th of November and it was not very likely — with their organisation and means of command that they were going to allow Guildford to be the only town in England without a bonfire on the wedding day of their future sovereign.

Forty Guys met in a field by the Merrow Road. Picking up timber from properties as they went they approached the town via Box Grove Road and London Road. They entered the town with torches, wearing their usual fantastic dress and carrying banners saying 'God Bless the Princess Alexandra' and 'Long Live the Queen'. Commenting on the meal for the old people and the lack of entertainment for the young, a third banner read '3rd Nation — All persons under 45 not to enjoy themselves on the 10th of March'. They made for Holy Trinity Church where they lit a bonfire in the High Street. The pro-Guy *West Surrey Times* reported:

> There was not much mischief in this . . . . Their conduct round the fire . . . was admirable. They had few fireworks; there were numerous ladies in the immediate proximity of the fire, and no

one had the slightest case for apprehension. Had it ended here all would have been well . . . but we regret to add that on their way to undress . . . they made a furious attack on Mr Eager's house . . . . What offence Mr Eager may have given them we do not know; but surely in a house where there may be women and children, to beat a man's windows with clubs, and smash his doorplate is not a manly or English mode of retaliation . . . . With good humour almost any licence may be allowed; but . . . let it be understood that if nothing is done by the authorities to provoke outrage, wanton attacks shall not be sanctioned by . . . the managers of these festivals . . . . We appeal to the good sense, and manly feeling of the 'Guys of Guildford' . . . . We trust that we shall see them in good spirits and good humour on the 5th of November next.

ST CATHERINE'S FAIR

Seven months later another incident occurred that brought the town into disrepute. The occasion for the trouble was St Catherine's Fair held every October. The fair itself was very tame. According to the *West Surrey Times* (10th October 1863) the weather was more suitable for 'ducks than human bipeds' and the mass of visitors were too shy to try the various fairground activities. 'The merry-go-rounds went round in a very tame way; and although those often headless, and always tail-less wooden horses never shy, the juveniles who patronised them were not of that rollicking and exuberant and demonstrative class that one generally meets with at these gatherings'. From coconut shies to gingerbread stalls business was bad. Even the recruiting sergeants were out of luck.

'Why do people go to these fairs?' asked the reporter from the *West Surrey Times*. He spied a grand old country gentleman with a 'clean smock frock, high crowned black beaver [hat], pearl buttoned waistcoat of marvellous and gaudy hue, neckcloth bright and variegated pattern, and gingham umbrella large enough to protect half the population of his parish from a passing shower'.

'Well, and so you've come to the fair then?' the reporter asked.

'Ees sir, ees sir-allus come to Cat-an-hill Fair — man and boy sir, I ha' cumd to Cat-an-hill Fair more nor sixty year'.

'What do you come for — to see the stalls and the shows?'

'Lor' bless'ee, no, sir. I used to care for them things once, but not now. But there be our Jane you see — she's at service wi' farmer Smith up this way; and there be our Mark, he's groom at parson's yonder; and there's Bill Styles and Tom Noakes, all on

St Catherine's Fair after J.M.W. Turner, 1832

'em used to belong to our parish, but they're spread about now; but I sees them all at Cat-an-hill Fair. And here's my missus . . . and them there's my grandchildren; and we all comes 'cos we sees and meets all our old friends like. Why all on 'em comes to Cat-an-hill. I wouldn't miss Cat-an-hill not if I knowed it — that I wouldn't'.

The reporter concluded, 'To meet old friends then appears to be one strong inducement for country folks to visit a fair. The force of habit and example too goes a long way with some, whilst the love of excitement or the marvellous attracts others'.

With the arrival of the evening, the fair livened up as more people came from the town. Tradesmen from as far away as Reading, Petworth and Farnham were busy selling rings, watches, gingerbread and all kinds of commodities. Large quantities of oysters on sale were swallowed, with effects the paper said were better 'imagined than described'.

One of the most popular attractions was a small caravan lit by naphtha flares claiming to be 'Manley's Museum of Science and Nature and Art'. On the stage outside the caravan was Mrs Manley, a stout red faced middle-aged woman in 'a remarkably low dress of dirty white muslin and scarlet trimmings'. She attracted a crowd with her efforts to dance to the strains of a set of bagpipes. Full of confidence, she proclaimed 'the most cleverest performance in all the fair; and if you wos to pay two shilluns in London you wouldn't see half so much . . . all for the low charge of one penny'. The next show was 'positively the last performance' as it had been since nine o'clock and continued to be until twelve o'clock. Inside the museum the talented Mrs Manley presented a 'pre-forming pony' and two 'pre-forming dogs' and what she called 'loger-de-many-hotherwise conjuring'. She impressed her audience by using her magic wand to convert a halfpenny, in a handkerchief held tightly by an urchin, into a half-crown. Handkerchiefs were torn to ribbons and restored to completion with a 'hey-presto' and a boy who was made to drink a potion usually reserved for chickens produced eggs from his elbow.

Another great attraction of the fair was no doubt the fact that, under an old charter, beer could be sold without a licence. The bountiful supply of drink got the better of some revellers. At one stall a man in an advanced state of inebriation played a dulcimer whilst his female companion beat a tambourine and collected money from people dancing round the stall. He would have fallen asleep had he not received an occasional wallop from the tambourine which put renewed life into the music. The dancers were about as sober as their accompanist. The *West Surrey Times* noted that:

> Stupid-looking fellows, many of them much advanced in beer and grinning like satyrs are figuring away with most marvellous steps, shuffling and double shuffling; whilst young women whose flushed faces, flashing eyes and bold demeanour plainly indicate that they also have imbibed far too freely, and whose sense of modesty and decorum appears to be rapidly vanishing under the excitement of the scene, are floundering about in the most execrable of crinolines to the immense satisfaction of the Satyrs aforesaid. This is the worst of the fair, and bad enough it is in all conscience. It effectively upsets all that can be said about 'innocent recreation for the masses'; for alas! there is little innocence here, and the preacher may preach in vain whilst these things exist to sap the morality and corrupt the virtue of the rural population.

It was no doubt people like this who had been responsible for bringing disgrace to the fair the previous week. Much to the embarrassment of those who ran the town the exploits of some of the locals reached the columns of *The Times* on 29th September 1863.

DISGRACEFUL PROCEEDINGS NEAR GUILDFORD
— Monday Evening — A riotous disturbance took place last
night, resulting in serious injury to upwards of 30 persons, at a
small village a mile from Guildford, known as St Catherine's
being at the foot of a high hill on the Guildford and Portsmouth
Road, on the summit of which is situated the ruined church of
St Catherine. It appears that on the 4th of October will recur
the annual fair of the village; and that on that day (Sunday) by
virtue of the old charter, the landlords of the village 'publics' are
allowed to draw beer even during prohibited hours. The Sunday
before the fair is known as 'Tap-up Sunday' and a similar
privilege is accorded. The village usually turns out in great
numbers, and some little licence is taken by them in throwing
chestnuts at passers-by, which generally creates a good deal of
merriment among the rustics, and has been good naturedly borne
by those who have been thus dealt with. This year the larking
has been carried on in a most inordinate manner. Yesterday
being 'Tap-up Sunday' upwards of 400 young fellows, many of
them being low characters of Guildford, assembled in the village,
lining the road on either side in formidable phalanx; and when
any peaceably inclined passenger approached they allowed him
or her to get into their midst; they then closed in and inflicted
both insult and injury. Mr Piggott, dyer, and his wife, were
driving through the village and were seriously hurt, Mrs Piggott
having her bonnet torn from her head. Mr Bailey, of the County
Magistrates' Clerk's Office, and his daughter were compelled to
go through a heavy shower of missiles; and the young lady is
still suffering from the effects of her fright. Mr Ellis, of
Farncombe, near Godalming, and two other gentlemen who were
in company with him were roughly handled; one having received
some bad wounds on his leg from kicks, and others having their
hats completely smashed and their coats torn to shreds. Miss
Chartres, of Brighton, Miss Smythe and several other ladies,
were rudely assaulted, one of them having her eye cut nearly out
by a stone whilst turning round to appeal to her assailants to
desist and the others either losing their shawls or other articles of
wearing apparel. Things got worse toward evening. Several
members of the county constabulary force made their appearance
on the scene; but this was only the signal for a still more riotous
demonstration than before; and it was considered advisable, even

St Catherine's Chapel, Guildford

for public safety, to leave the mob to their own course, and to prevent them from having further victims by placing the police at convenient distances from the village and cautioning passengers against going on the turnpike road and inducing them to pursue, for their own personal saftey's sake, their journey by the river bank instead, though more circuitous. Several fugitives from the insults of the mob were pursued, however, notwithstanding this precautionary measure; and more than one case occurred in which persons who were pursued down the lane from St Catherine's Hill were forcibly pushed into the water. At nightfall nothing could restrain the fury of the crowd. Mr Shrubb, a resident of the Portsmouth Road, was incautious enough to appeal to the better sense of the roughs, if they had any; but he was at once hushed by the loud groans they set up, and assailed with a shower of stones. They next proceeded to his residence, pulled up the whole of the palings of his property, and conveyed it to the top of St Catherine's whence they went to the cutting between the two tunnels on the London and South-Western line of the railway, where they carried off all the wooden railings they could get at, and afterwards lighted a huge bonfire which was seen at a long distance on the surrounding hills of the county. Much other injury was done to both person and property, which has not as yet been officially reported. The county constabulary under Mr Superintendent Parr are diligently making every inquiry so as to bring the ringleaders of the disturbance to justice and we have just heard that two or three men have been taken into custody. Should not the chief promoters of these disgraceful transactions be committed, it is feared that the usual demonstrations in this town on the coming anniversary of Gunpowder Plot will assume a still more riotous aspect than they have hitherto been wont.

The following day there was a leader in *The Times*:

It makes matters worse that there does not seem to have been any ground, either political or religious animosity, for such wholesale savagery . . . . The riot appears to have been due to nothing but wanton mischievousness and cruelty . . . . The whole blame for the outbreak must be laid on the authorities and the police. The fault is entirely theirs for allowing the mob to get such head. There are roughs enough everywhere, if they were given free play, to endanger the public peace and to make passengers afraid of their lives . . . . Guildford is peculiarly unhappy, not in its inhabitants, but in its authorities. We believe indeed, that the town has for some time past been the scene of similar disgraceful outbreaks on the 5th of November; but this only shows that the authorities have for some time past been disgracefully lax . . . . We cannot conceive of any excuse sufficient to exonerate the authorities. They have ample powers to put down any such breaches of the peace . . . . If neither the borough nor the county police are able to keep the peace and secure the freedom of the highway it would be well if the SECRETARY OF STATE for the Home Department . . . were to take such steps as would remedy the evil, and at the same time make the ratepayers of the borough pay heavily for his assistance.

This savage attack on the town spurred both the inhabitants and the authorities into a flurry of letter writing. On 30th September Captain Hastings, the Chief Constable of the Surrey Constabulary wrote to the Home Office, playing down the situation:

No one as far as the police have been able to ascertain received any serious injury whatsoever. The whole affair was really of so trivial and unimportant a character that had it not been for the grossly exaggerated account which has appeared in one or two of the London newspapers and which has called forth a leader in *The Times* of this day, I should not have thought it necessary to trouble the Secretary of State with a report of the matter.

In conclusion I beg to say that I have made arrangements for the preservation of the peace on Sunday next, in the event of any attempt being made to repeat a similar disturbance.

On the matter of the sale of beer at the fair, the Home Office informed Hastings that Acts of Parliament prohibiting the sale of beer without a licence overruled the old charter said to have been granted to St Catherine's in the reign of Henry VII. Hastings replied on 28th November:

St Catherine's from Guildford

I have the honour to acknowledge the receipt of your letter of 24th instant in which you refer to certain Acts of Parliament prohibiting the sale of beer without a licence and further requesting that I inform Sir George Grey on what grounds it is contended that the sale of beer without a licence at the Fair at St Catherine's Hill does not fall within the provisions of the Acts.

In reply I beg to state for the information of Sir George Grey that it has been the custom, for a great number of years so far as I have been able to ascertain for any inhabitant of the Parish to sell beer without a licence on the two days of the fair which is held annually at St Catherine's Hill. . . .

In future, however, I shall give our notice that the said practice will no longer be permitted and that any person so offending will be summoned before the magistrates.

Letters were also sent by inhabitants of the town to the Home Office and to *The Times*. Three rather nervous old ladies wrote to the Home Office on 5th October:

As the 5th of November is near at hand it is highly desirable that some means more efficient that the ordinary constabulary appliances, which are confessedly insufficient should be brought into operation to prevent a recurrence of the disgraceful disturbances which have so repeatedly stigmatised the town and placed its peaceably disposed inhabitants in the utmost terror and it would be some satisfaction to these to know that Her Majesty's Government, of which you are the Home Secretary, are intending to take special steps to this end.

Another frustrated inhabitant, Mr Browe, had this to say:

Englishmen, far away from their country, can look to the British Government for protection and redress, when their property is destroyed by a riotous mob. Shall we not enjoy the same privilege at home, under the very shadow of the throne of our beloved Queen?

CHAPTER IX

THE END

HAD 1863 not seen a Royal Wedding and had the town not made the national press, one wonders how the town authorities would have tackled the Guys. Would they have adopted the same inadequate measures chosen by their predecessors in the 1850s? Was extension of mischief to other parts of the year the turning point or did it merely reinforce the determination of the authorities to stop the riots? The answer is not clear but faced with so much criticism the Mayor realised that action had to be taken and so he opened a lengthy dialogue with the Home Office. On 5th October Mr Piper requested an interview with the Home Secretary. He said that the riots the previous year had been so terrible that he was resolved to do something. The interview took place and on 14th October Mr Piper wrote to the Home Secretary explaining his plans. He would swear in special constables and would organise a force to guard the ammunition in the militia depot. He also requested a couple of detectives and some metropolitan policemen as the Chief Constable of Surrey Constabulary refused to release any of the county police. The Home Office, however, was not prepared to lend any metropolitan police and advised the Mayor to approach the military authorities at Aldershot for some troops. This the Mayor did and the town braced itself for Bonfire Night. The local police and the special constables would try to maintain order and some troops would be stationed on the edge of town in case the situation became uncontrollable. The atmosphere remained tense right up to 5th November. Two days before Bonfire Night Piper received word that the Guys planned to anticipate the arrival of the troops and so the army was immediately dispatched to the town. Lt. Col. Gray led 150 men of the 37th Foot and 50 men of the 1st Royal Dragoons into the town at 10.40pm. Inhabitants usually came out to watch the arrival of troops but Gray was struck by the peculiar quiet in the town. It seemed to confirm a report of a countryman that a meeting was being held on the Downs to plan some mischief to forestall the arrival of the troops. Gray expected that the Guys would either light a bonfire outside the town on Bonfire Night or would wait until the army left. Meanwhile *The Times* kept the town in the national limelight with an article on 6th November:

GUY FAWKES DAY AT GUILDFORD

GUILDFORD THURSDAY — A representation was recently made to Sir George Grey hoping that some steps would be taken to prevent a recurrence of the riotous proceedings which have annually taken place in Guildford on the 5th, and one ground for the prayer was the alleged inefficiency of the local authorities to suppress such disturbances. Sir George accordingly placed himself in communication with the Mayor, Mr. Henry Piper, and as a result of such conference, measures were at once taken to aid the police. This was the more necessary as up to the last moment it was announced that, whatever opposition might be offered by the local authorities the Guys had resolved not to be deprived of their accustomed bonfire and procession.

The rumours which have been current during the last few days have of course been greatly exaggerated, but the surprise of nearly everybody was complete to see on Wednesday morning not fewer that 50 Dragoons and 150 men of the 37th Regiment marching to their quarters at the various public houses in the town. The former had come in by road on the previous night, under the command of Captain Robertson, and the latter arrived by special train from Aldershot, via Tongham, under Lieutenant-Colonel Gray. Upwards of 160 special constables had also been sworn in, and the two local corps of Rifle Volunteers, the 13th and 24th, were also ordered to be ready to assist in preserving the peace. The county constabulary under Mr. Superintendent

Parr and Mr. Inspector Barker, have had supplementary forces to prevent any outbreak beyond the jurisdiction of the borough authorities. It was at first intended to have a number of the metropolitan 'A' reserve police but these have not yet arrived.

The Guys had determined to anticipate the authorities by holding their lark on Tuesday night. But their purpose was discovered. The authorities at once ordered into the town the military, who had, indeed, been in readiness ever since Sunday to come away from Aldershot at any moment. The soldiers were kept for an hour on the Farnham Road, near the New County Hospital, not knowing if they should be ordered to actual service immediately on their arrival. The rumour that the soldiers were within a few yards of the entrance to the town had the effect of preventing any attempt to form a procession; but, as it was, the military were received with yells and other cries similar to those in which the Guys usually enter the town. A number of squibs and crackers were thrown among them, but no personal injury was sustained.

Today the town is in a state of great excitement. The special constables are under orders. The whole of the High Street, from the Ram Inn at the top of the town, to the bridge leading to the railway station, is to be kept by military, and every avenue leading from other parts of the town into the High Street is to be guarded, so that the Guys are this year prevented from making, as usual, a bonfire opposite Trinity Church. Mr. Superintendent Vickers and the borough police force are under orders to take into custody every person either shouting, letting off squibs, or in any other way inciting a breach of the peace.

While we are writing (8 o'clock) it is reported that the Guys have pitched upon three spots, close to but outside the borough, where they intend to have their usual bonfire, if possible; and this evening a number of names have transpired of respectable townsmen who are 'marked' as victims on the first possible opportunity. Some of these have wisely barricaded their houses, to preserve their windows from destruction; and few of the peaceable inhabitants are disregarding the Mayor's published caution to remain within doors. A large number of 'roughs' are about but as yet (8 o'clock) no cases of serious damage or injury have been reported to the police authorities. The rumour still runs afloat that as soon as the military are withdrawn the rioters will 'come out stronger than ever', but it is doubtless competent for the local authorities to retain the police and military force now at their command so long as any fear of outbreak is apprehended.

GUILDFORD, FRIDAY — After the time at which we wrote (8 o'clock) on Thursday evening the original intention to have the soldiery out to guard the whole of the High Street from the invasion of the roughs was departed from but they were held in readiness to appear at any given moment to quell any actual disturbance should the efforts of the large number of special constables who had been sworn in have proved unavailing. Things were quiet until a little after 10 o'clock when signs of an approaching row were very evident. Several bands of roughs promenaded up and down, yelling and hooting, and in spite of the prohibition of fireworks by the magistrates, there were many squibs and crackers let off in the very faces of the constabulary. One or two lads were apprehended, and in one case a rescue was attempted. This was prevented by the timely assistance of the special constables. The lads were taken before the Mayor who cautioned and afterwards discharged them. The Mayor, Mr Henry Piper, with the Town Clerk, Mr Smallpiece and other local authorities were at the Town Hall during the evening. About quarter past 10 o'clock there were three attempts made to make bonfires in the streets. That in front of Holy Trinity Church, which was always accounted the principal one, was speedily prevented. The second was a little more successful, in Chapel Street but the special constables soon arrived on the spot, and trampled out the embers. Here a collision with the mob was imminent and only prevented by the arrival of a second force of constables. The third was lighted on the steep hill leading to the cemetery [Mount Street]. This was blazing for some little time before it was noticed but a number of the special constables went to the spot and speedily extinguished it. A row occurred opposite the Angel Hotel, and it really appeared as if extraordinary measures would have to be taken to put it down. A shower of stones was sent at the constables and one of them, Mr Hart, painter, was badly hurt. It was here deemed advisable to give the usual public caution. The Mayor and the Town Clerk accordingly proceeded from the Town Hall. Standing on the steps in front of the Angel Hotel, the latter deliberately read the Riot Act and the Mayor ordered the streets to be cleared. The special constables then formed in a compact body, and drawing their truncheons marched down the street, driving all before them. Several cases of personal injury occurred but none were serious. The Mayor and other local authorities remained at the Town Hall until nearly 1 o'clock this morning, when the streets had become less crowded, but it was considered desirable that military pickets should be on duty up and down the High Street all night until daybreak today. One or two bonfires were lighted in private gardens, but of course the police had no power to interfere with these. A party of Guildford roughs, it was said, went over to Godalming, finding their efforts here were abortive, and created a good deal of trouble. A huge bonfire was blazing away there as early as 7 o'clock in the evening. There were also bonfires at Shalford, Chilworth, Gomshall, Dorking and other places bordering on the South-Eastern line of the railway. It is said that the Guys are determined on the first possible occasion to have their bonfire and masked procession, but any attempt to carry out this purpose will be promptly suppressed.

Unlike *The Times* the pro-Guy *West Surrey Times* was incensed by the precautions taken and attacked the authorities on 7th November.

A more unconstitutional proceeding in a free country we never heard of in all our lives. . . . What have the magistrates done? In a moment of panic they have actually brought into the town a troop of 200 soldiers, cavalry and infantry, to keep in awe some 30 or 40 young fellows. . . . There are magistrates on the County Bench who have co-operated with the Guys and them- selves been Guys, and there are solicitors both in Guildford and Godalming, who have given money to the Guys. . . . We have sought to make the proceedings of the 5th of November the sort of harmless but merry rejoicing, in which everyone might participate without fear; the townspeople who reside near the spot where the bonfire is usually kindled sitting at their windows, and inviting their friends to come and view the spectacle. If the authorities had aided us in this, the 5th of November in Guildford would have been one of the most enjoyable days in the whole year. Instead of this our magistrates . . . have pursued their own particular notions . . .until they have brought things in the town to the present pass.

The *West Surrey Times* was highly critical of the use of the Riot Act and even questioned the legality of the Mayor's actions. One problem with the Act was that it failed to adequately define what constituted a riot and on this occasion it was questionable as to whether a riot was taking place. The crowd were not given one hour to disperse as required by the Act before the special constables cleared the streets. Reflecting on the injuries caused by the 'specials' the *West Surrey Times* concluded:

We cannot but think that the Borough Magistrates have exhibited a great want of discretion. And where, we ask, is all this to end? Animosities have, we fear, been kindled which it will be difficult to quell, and we doubt whether wise and conciliatory advice will now have any effect upon persons who have been thus unnecessarily exasperated.

This show of force by the authorities was a big risk. What would happen when the troops left? It was not going to be a problem for Mr Piper, however, because a new Mayor was elected a few days after Bonfire Night. He inherited the reins of a town on the verge of crisis but was one of the few men strong-minded enough to save it. According to Henry Peak 'there was . . . at that time, a gentleman residing in the Woodbridge Road, named Philip Whittington Jacob; he was a man of learning, a great linguist, acquainted with the Sanskrit and other ancient tongues, but also a man of great force of character. . . . It was determined by the Town Council to invite Mr Jacob to serve the office of Mayor with a free hand to put down the disgraceful proceedings'. Superintendent Law, who was to help Jacob, recalled that 'on the 9th November of that year Mr Jacob was elected Mayor for the first

SOME RELICS.

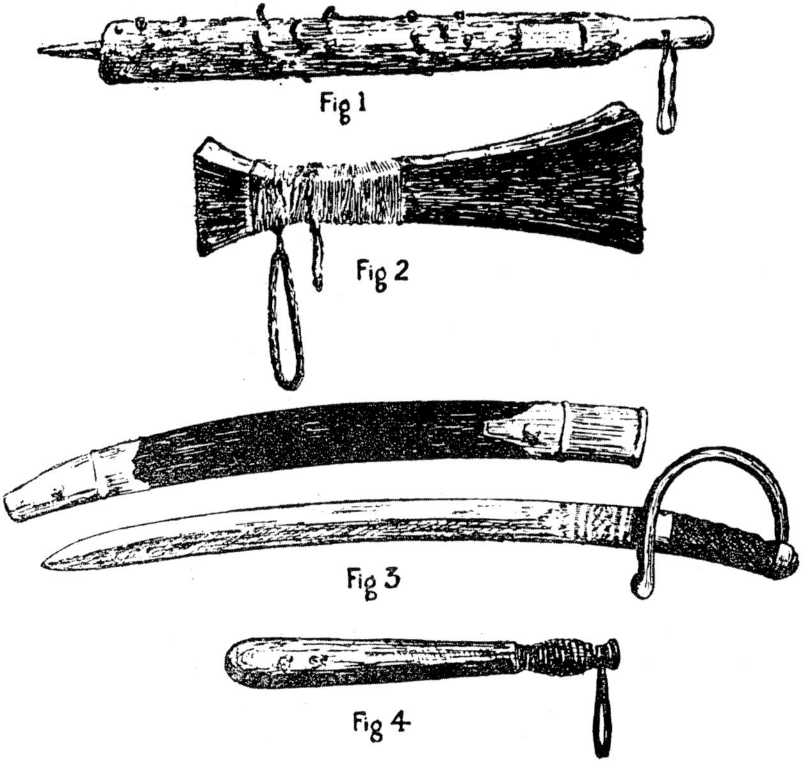

Fig 1

Fig 2

Fig 3

Fig 4

Fig 1.—*A weapon captured from the Guys now in Guildford Museum.*
Fig 2.—*A weapon of a Guildford Trader.*
Fig 3.—*A police cutlass.*
Fig 4.—*An official staff.*

time. He was well known to be a man of great determination and possibly that had something to do with his selection'. At his maiden speech to the Councillors as Mayor, reported in the *West Surrey Times*, Jacob expressed his determination to tackle the riots. He thanked the councillors for electing him. He had a great objection to being elected on account of his health and was afraid that this might prevent him from attending all the meetings. But if it pleased God to give him health he would promise them that any defect or shortcoming should not be from want of zeal. He especially asked for their help to end the troubles on 5th November. He was sure that a great deal was to be done by individual influence and public feeling, perhaps more than by force of law. He hoped that they would endeavour to influence their friends and persuade them to withdraw their countenance from such proceedings in every possible way. There were many who looked upon the Fifth as a matter of amusement and who regarded the plundering of fences as a trivial matter but the time had come when it must be stopped. He believed that everyone in the town would say that such a state of things could not go on any longer. He hoped that those who had in any way sanctioned these riots hitherto would now see that it was time for their sanction to be withdrawn, and would endeavour to put them down energetically. If put down by force of moral opinion it would be much better; but if it were not achieved in that way other means must be employed.

Jacob's first problem was how to secure the town against the Guys once the army left. The troops were due to leave the town on 11th November so Jacob asked the Home Office if they could stay until he had made provision for the defence of the town. His plans reveal great attention to detail. 151 'specials' were sworn in on 18th November in addition to the 50 special constables sworn in annually. The town was divided into districts and a list was made of the special constables in each, grouped in the order by which they could be most conveniently summoned. The police were to keep an eye open for any indications of a riot, and in an emergency were to use the Town Hall bell to summon all 'specials' within earshot. The Home Office permitted the troops to stay but warned that they could not remain on a long-term basis and would have to leave by the 18th or 19th November. Jacob argued that he needed longer but he failed to convince the Home Office. On 19th November the army left and abandoned Guildford to its fate.

Two days later on 21st November the Guys arrived. At eleven o'clock on that Saturday evening the sound of 'loo, loo' was heard from the direction of Stoke Road. Between fifteen and twenty Guys, grotesquely dressed entered the High Street accompanied by a crowd. They made for the shop of Mr Weale, draper and magistrate, and hammered at the strong shutters protecting his ground floor. They then went to the police station where they savagely beat up P.C. Sutton who very nearly died from his injuries. Then they returned to Mr Weale's, where they managed to tear down a shutter and smashed a plate-glass window. They pelted the upper windows and smashed all of them on the first floor. Next they dashed along the High Street and Spital Street and attacked the house of Mr Hart, a veterinary surgeon. They broke several windows in his sitting room and knocked him to the ground when he came to the door. He picked himself up and struck his assailant but was again knocked down. The next target was the home of Mr Piper in the Merrow Road, where the Guys smashed all the windows at the front of the house.

The attack had lasted less than half an hour. The Guys took off their costumes and abandoned them at the Union Workhouse as they disappeared into the night. As they were leaving the Town Hall bell was rung and between forty and fifty special constables left their beds to answer the call. Mr Jacob, the Mayor, rushed to the scene and read the Riot Act. The specials divided into three groups and patrolled the town until half past two when most of them were dismissed by Jacob. The militia were also mustered and remained in the town, armed, until half past twelve, but the damage had been done. The town had been taken completely by surprise and the specials found the streets empty save a few spectators. The *West Surrey Times* reporting the attack sympathised with the victims but it still clung to the belief that none of this would have happened had the town decided to support the traditional Bonfire Night celebrations.

On the morning after the trouble (Sunday 22nd November) the Borough Magistrates met to discuss the situation. Jacob wrote to the Home Office, asking for detectives to be sent to the town, and he announced that a reward had been offered for the apprehension of the offenders. On Monday a proclamation was published and printed in the *West Surrey Times* later that week:

P.C. Sutton

£100 Reward — Whereas on the night of Saturday, the 21st of November instant, certain evil-disposed persons assembled, and with great violence attacked and partly demolished the houses of Mr Henry Piper and Mr Joseph Weale, situate in the Borough of Guildford, and also ill-treated and abused Police Constable Sutton, so as to place his life in danger. Notice is hereby given that the above reward will be paid to any persons giving such information as shall lead to the conviction of any of the perpetrators of these outrages. All information to be given to Mr G.F. Vickers, Superintendent of Police at Guildford, by whom the reward will be paid.

Guildford, 23rd November, 1863,

Later that day more handbills were printed announcing that the reward had been increased to £200. A letter was received from the Home Office offering a further £50 reward and a pardon to any Guys who gave information. On Tuesday another proclamation was printed:

£250 Reward, and Her Majesty's Free Pardon — In addition to the £200 already offered for the conviction of the perpetrators of the late outrages in this town, a further reward of £50 will be given by Her Majesty's Government to such persons as shall give information and evidence which shall lead to the conviction of any of the persons who were engaged in the outrages. A free pardon will also be granted to any accomplice, not being one of those engaged in the felonious assault on the constable, who shall give such evidence as shall lead to the same result. Information to be given to Mr G. F. Vickers, Superintendent of Police at Guildford.

Guildford, 24th November 1863,

Rumours circulated the town suggesting that the Guys would make another attack. On the Tuesday night special constables waited at Lacelles Brewery until three or four in the morning but the Guys never came. Gossips spread stories that detectives were in the town. One was of a man claiming to be a bricklayer looking for work, who blew his cover when he entered pubs begging. He held out his hands and revealed palms that were as soft as a lady's.

The next task for Jacob was the reorganisation of the local police force. Captain Hastings of the county police force agreed to find a suitable superintendent for the borough force. Superintendent Vickers had been in charge of the town's three policemen since 1855 but Jacob planned a complete shake-up. On 26th November the Town Council agreed to the appointment of nine extra constables which effectively doubled the expenditure on the borough force. The councillors also gave Jacob permission to dismiss Vickers and appoint whoever he wished. On the following morning Jacob called on Captain Hastings at the county police station. Hastings looked down the list of men under his supervision and put his finger on the name John Henry Law.

'That is the best man we have', remarked Superintendent Parr who was also present.

'Then he is just the man you want', Hastings said turning to Jacob. Law was stationed at Witley and quickly presented himself to the county police station where the offer of Superintendent of the Guildford Police Force was made to him.

'If I go into the borough under these circumstances', he said to Jacob, 'I shall want the support of the magistrates'.

'Yes, Mr Law', replied Jacob, 'I can assure you that you will have the full support of the magistrates and myself as well'.

Superintendent Vickers pre-empted his dismissal and resigned. He cleared out of the station house the week beginning Sunday 29th November, and Law moved in on the following Tuesday. Meanwhile the Guys were expected at any time. A special constable recorded in his diary that he was out on Monday 7th December until about one o'clock the following morning. On the Wednesday the Guys were again expected and he recorded that about sixty

John Henry Law

Guys actually met and dressed. Once they realised that they were expected they delayed their arrival until midnight.

It cannot have been long after this that the 'specials' were paid off since Law recalled that their dismissal was the first thing he did on taking up his position. He also asked for some more uniformed men. On 11th December the Watch Committee agreed to the appointment of another six policemen, bringing the total number of borough police to twelve (according to Law). Law also decided to arm his men with cutlasses. The Town Clerk took the precaution of informing the Home Office of this move in a letter dated 15th December. Superintendent Law trained his men hard and insisted on tight discipline:

> My instructions to the police under me were: 'When the order is given, if any man attempts to turn back, let his comrade cut him down!' . . . I drilled the men myself, being greatly assisted by P.C. Cook, who had been a sergeant in a cavalry regiment. I also drilled with the men so as to encourage them. It was quite surprising to see how well the men went through their drill — they did it splendidly. When the next November came — that would be in 1864 — several attempts were made by the roughs to get into the town and commit their usual outrages, but their attempts were prevented.

November 5th 1864 past quietly in the town. Only a few squibs and crackers were fired at a respectful distance from the police. The *Surrey Advertiser* felt that the frosty weather and the cutlasses carried by the police discouraged people from venturing out. It decided, however, that the main reason for the peace was that 'the working men of Guildford mindful of the self-respect that is expected of the working man in these progressive days turned a deaf ear to those who called for disturbances'. The Guys stayed out of the town and lit two fires at the Rifle Range of the 13th Surrey Volunteers on the Farnham Downs. The flames could be seen at a great distance. One of the Surrey Volunteers recorded in his diary:

At ten minutes to ten o'clock there were reflections of two great fires on the Farnham Downs. They turned out to be the butts at our range, set on fire by the mob. Went to the Town Hall and volunteered as a special constable.

There he discovered the Mayor and about sixty other 'specials'. They divided into threes and patrolled different parts of the district but no trouble occurred. Law took some policemen to the rifle range and dispersed the mob there. In the weeks that followed a visit from the Guys was continually expected. The Surrey volunteer wrote in his diary that on Tuesday 13th December 1864 he 'marched to Wonersh with the corps. Stopped at Mr Fentums a short time. Had bread, cheese and ale. We then marched home and found that the townspeople had been expecting a visit from the Guys, who were near upon taking advantage of our absence, but they were found out by the police before they were ready'.

The following year (1865) the Guys came out on 1st November. About thirty Guys dressed in their usual costumes came out of a lane by the side of the church carrying palings from a house in School Lane. They dumped their load in the High Street, poured fuel over the pile and set it alight. Superintendent Law was in the lower part of the High Street giving instructions to Acting Sergeant Titley when he saw the flames. He ran to the police station grabbed his cutlass and rushed to the fire with a few men. The Guys dancing round the flames fled and Law extinguished the flames. At the bottom of the fire he found a 2-gallon can of petroleum which had not ignited. He dragged it out and took it to the police station.

The incident was minor compared with what usually happened. There was no grand procession as in previous years. The *Surrey Advertiser* claimed the bonfire was just a harmless lark that one should expect at election time. The town was becoming complacent. Henry Peak recalled that 'the townspeople who had to pay heavily [for the precautions against the Guys] became weary of the proceedings, felt that the noisy element had been crushed and that it was

safe to look upon the matter as ended'. *The Times* for 12th
November 1864 published a letter from an inhabitant of Guildford
who expressed the view that the riots were over. He also revealed
the effects that Guildford's reputation for lawlessness had had on
the town.

> Sir — A year since you commented in strong terms on the
> riots which disgraced this town and greatly alarmed its peaceable
> inhabitants your notice has had its effect. We have obtained a
> bad name; strangers have fought shy of us, houses have remained
> unlet, and many of our householders who were accustomed to
> let lodgings have had their rooms much more frequently empty
> than on previous years.
>
> In this way the town has suffered. I do not write this in a
> complaining spirit, and fully admit the force and justice of your
> article. In fact, the absolute necessity of effective measures,
> however difficult and expensive to carry out, to restore peace,
> the due observance of the law, and respectability of the town was
> only too evident to all the townspeople.
>
> I feel you will be gratified to hear that thanks to the unwearied
> and vigourous exertions of our most able Mayor, Mr. P.W.
> Jacob, aided by the magistrates and council of the borough, and
> supported by a largely increased force and an active inspector
> (the police being very properly armed with cutlasses), the hitherto
> riotous 5th of November passed without any disturbance in the
> borough.
>
> The inhabitants may now hope that they are altogether deliv-
> ered from the violent display of mob law, or rather lawlessness,
> under which they have so long suffered.
>
> I need not say a notice of our present improved state in *The
> Times* would greatly benefit the town, by restoring confidence to
> those who may contemplate living in or visiting it, and also by
> removing the stigma under which greatly to our loss, both in
> profit and in character, we have remained during the past year.

I am, sir, your obedient servant,

A RATEPAYER
Guildford, 11th November

The Town Council was also feeling confident that peace had been restored and was keen to reduce the expenditure on the police force. Jacob, however, disagreed. He hoped, when the proper time arrived, to be able to 'reduce the force but he thought it bad economy to do so until the riots were kept down, which injured the town to a large extent and gave it a bad name'. Far from being a harmless lark, Jacob believed the 'disgraceful occurrence' on 1st November was an indication that trouble could still break out. And, far from wanting to reduce the force Jacob wanted to invest more money in it to increase its efficiency. He asked the Town Council if they would sanction an increase in the pay of the two first-class constables by a shilling a week to 23s. This measure would amount to an extra £5 4s a year and Jacob needed to encourage the men since it was very hard to get recruits who could be trained. Many had to be dismissed for drunkeness and misconduct and consequently Jacob had seen thirty men pass through the police force during his time as Mayor. Jacob's request was not greeted with enthusiasm. Councillor Cooke was very sorry to hear the Mayor state his determination not to reduce the police force. He hoped events would make the Mayor reconsider. The frank discussion that followed revealed that Jacob's campaign to bring peace to the town involved struggles within the Council Chamber as well as on the streets. The councillors were either totally naive, having learnt nothing from the battles with the Guys in the past or, as is more likely, they were blinded to reality by their efforts to cut expenditure:

Councillor Holt: Does the Mayor ask this increase for twelve months?

The Mayor: I ask to raise the pay of the first-class constables.

Mr Williamson: I think the public opinion is against any such increase, and I shall oppose it if it is intended to extend over a period of twelve months. I shall support the increase if it is restricted to three months. (Hear, hear).

The Mayor:	All I ask is to allow a shilling a week extra to the first-class constables.
Mr Holt:	I have no objection to giving them 1s. extra but I want to reduce the force in another three months.
The Mayor:	You must understand that there is a great deal of difficulty in getting good men.
Mr Cooke:	I suppose the best men stay with you the longest?
The Mayor:	Of course they do.
Mr Lovett:	Can the Town Clerk tell the present expenditure for the police force?
Mr Smallpiece:	It is £714; and you get a portion of that back.
Mr Lovett:	I think it is very desirable to see whether we cannot reduce this expenditure for the police force. (Hear, hear.) A sum of £714 is a large amount when you consider it is raised out of the pockets of the burgesses. I am quite sure the Town Council will render to the Mayor every support in establishing a good and sufficient police force for the preservation of the peace in the borough. But it seems to me that a large force of fifteen or sixteen men. . . .
The Mayor:	Twelve constables, a sergeant and super-intendent.
Mr Lovett:	Well that is a very large number. It appears to me that if eight men cannot keep down riotous proceedings in the town, it is impossible for sixteen men to do it. I should say with all the volunteers at our command. . . .

The Mayor:	We cannot call out volunteers to act in such a way.
Mr Lovett:	Well, we have the special constables. I certainly do hope with Mr Cooke, that the expediency of reducing the force will be considered.
The Mayor:	You cannot expect the special constables to patrol the streets at night. On the night of the 1st inst. the principal part of the force was at the lower part of the town. If it is your pleasure to reduce the police force, of course, do so but it will be a bad economy, for you will gain shillings and lose pounds. (Hear, hear.)
Mr Boxall:	I propose that the consideration of the question be postponed until the quarterly meeting of the Council in February.
The Mayor:	Well, gentlemen, no one is more anxious than I to lighten the burthen of the public; but that little affair the other night showed me the spirit which still exists — and so strongly that it only wants an opportunity of breaking out.

Mr Jacob was right. On Monday 18th December eighteen Guys lit a bonfire outside Dudley House. A policeman saw them and when he blew his whistle they ran away up the Portsmouth Road. Eight days later more trouble occurred. It was Boxing Day and in the afternoon a crowd of between 150 and 200 people marched up the High Street singing and shouting, two men carrying on their shoulders a man sitting in a chair. The crowd was good-humoured and dispersed when asked by Superintendent Law.

Later that night, however, the most vicious battle of the Guys era occurred. Perhaps as a result of the afternoon's proceedings Law had several men on duty in the High Street. Soon after eight o'clock about fifteen to twenty Guys entered the town armed with great bludgeons, poles and stones and dressed fiercesomely. One wore an old military-style cocked hat, cord trousers and a white shirt over his coat. Another wore an oilskin cap over his head with eyeholes cut out; his coat was worn inside out and his trousers were rolled up to his knees. A third wore a long white shirt rolled up to his waist with the arms rolled up and a cotton handkerchief on his head pulled down to cover part of his face. Their appearance was designed to terrorise their victims and their first victim was P.C. Stent.

Sergt. Titley　　　　　　　　　　*P.C. Davis*

At 8.20pm Stent was standing on the crest of the town bridge. He recognised the man in the cocked hat as Reeves, a local ruffian he had met three months before. Only a few weeks before Christmas, Reeves had run up behind Stent in the High Street and struck him on the face. On this evening Reeves clutched a thick pole about 4-feet long. On seeing Stent, the Guys cried

'Whoo' and hurled stones. Stent took to his heels and was pursued up the High Street. P.C. Castleman was at the foot of the bridge and managed to hide in a gateway. He saw the Guys rush passed shouting. One of their missiles hit Stent and then Reeves rushed ahead of the others and clubbed the policeman to the ground.

'Kill him! Kill him!' cried the others as another Guy struck Stent, 'Murder the b-----'.

Stent lay on the ground with his head bleeding while the man in the oilskin mask gave him a final blow but by now other policemen were drawing the attention of the gang.

P.C. Watts had been near the corner of Quarry Street when he saw the angry mob charging in his direction. Grabbing his whistle he ran up the High Street sounding the alarm. P.C. Marshall ran down from Swan Lane and met Sergeant Titley and P.C Davis, who ran from Star Corner to join Watts. With their cutlasses drawn they hastily formed a line as a shower of stones fell on them, followed by an assault of poles and bludgeons. P.C. Marshall was cut badly by a blow from Reeves and fell on his knees. A second blow from another Guy smashed his helmet and knocked him to the ground. P.C. Watts managed to parry a pole, dived under it and struck his attacker but being outnumbered he too was knocked down. As he lay on the ground trying to protect his head from more blows, he saw Reeves rush at Sergeant Titley. Titley fended off the full force of a blow to his stomach whilst another Guy struck at P.C. Davis who successfully guarded off the weapon aimed at his head. Another policeman, P.C. Braddon, came down the High Street to help. He saw P.C. Davis disarm his attacker. Sergeant Titley managed to knock the pole out of Reeves's hands. Then all of a sudden the Guys fled. The police training had paid off and they ran after them. Sergeant Titley chased Reeves down Mill Lane but lost sight of him in Millmead. P.C. Braddon however caught up with the Guy in the oilskin mask near Millmead Bridge and knocked him down with his cutlass. P.C. Watts arrived to find the two men struggling and helped

Braddon take the Guy, whose name was Nugent, to the police station. Watts then went with P.C. Davis in search of other Guys. At the bottom of the High Street they saw two men running over the bridge. P.C. Watts noticed that they had come from the

A Policeman faces Rioters

direction of Millmead. Both were exhausted but not wearing any costume. P.C. Davis recognised one of them as the man he had disarmed. His name was Stevens.

'You are one of the men I want', Watts said to him.

'I don't know anything about it', replied Stevens.

'What will my poor wife do?' whined the other man, virtually crying. His name was Pearson and he was taken into custody with Stevens.

The descriptions of the attack suggest that Reeves was the leader of the mob. He had escaped in Millmead but foolishly returned to the High Street. The circumstances of his capture as recorded in the *Surrey Advertiser* seem very strange and suggest he was possibly drunk. At a quarter to nine he met a William Bakewell who was walking down the High Street and told him that he would 'pull the b----- town down'.

'Pull the town down if you like but don't insult me', replied Bakewell. Reeves then threatened to pull Bakewell's 'b----- house down'.

'If you don't run I'll give you in charge', warned Bakewell, threatening to have Reeves arrested.

Reeves did not run but continued threatening to pull down and burn Bakewell's house so Bakewell fetched a policeman from the White Lion Hotel. By the end of the evening, then, four men had been arrested. P.C. Stent survived his ordeal and was taken to Waller Martin's shop in the High Street near where he fell. Dr Eager was called and found him in agony bleeding profusely from hideous wounds to his eye and forehead.

Edwin Reeves, cooper, aged 26, William Nugent, painter, aged 29, George Stevens, painter, aged 23, and John Pearson, coachsmith's labourer were taken before the Kingston Assizes. The charge of intent to murder was dismissed and all the charges against Pearson were withdrawn. On 7th April Lord Chief Baron sentenced Reeves and Nugent to twelve months hard labour for rioting and causing bodily harm. Stevens was guilty of rioting only and received three months' hard labour.

'Ah, Mr Law', said one of the four as the Superintendent took him to prison, 'there'll never be no more Guildford Riots'. And there never were.

CHAPTER X

EPILOGUE

And now, happily, I can add, that never since has there been riot or unlawful proceedings of any sort, but Guildford has long ago recovered its right to the title of a law-abiding and well-ordered town, and those who are left of its old inhabitants honour the memory of Philip Whittington Jacob.

Henry Peak, 1902

Up to November 1863 there were many people, even some of wealth and influence who thought that November 5th ought to be observed and who rather than give up the old custom were willing to put up with — to connive at — a certain amount of riot, mischief and damage to property. But after the outbreak occurred in that month when a number of misguided men came out suddenly not for a lark, not for anything that could possibly be called fun, or amusement, but to do as much mischief as possible, when they attacked and greatly damaged the houses of two men, who so far from being objects of hatred and dislike, were greatly respected both for their private character and the good which they had been doing in the town for many years that those persons felt they could no longer countenance men who were guilty of such abominable outrage and instead of thwarting and opposing the efforts of the magistrates to put down the riots were rather inclined to help them.

I am convinced that one great reason why there has been no disturbance on 5th November during the past four years and so little at other times has been the knowledge that a body of courageous energetic men, interested in preserving order, were ready to come out at a moments notice to assist the police to resist the rioters and I think therefore that a considerable share of the credit due to suppression of the rioters belongs to them and that I should have found it very difficult, if not impossible, to accomplish what was done without their assistance.

P. W. Jacob in the *Surrey Advertiser* 21st March 1868

Upon various occasions and for different reasons...crowds of people gathered together in the town and when this happened it would invariably terminate in a fight. Is it due to stricter surveillance that this is not so now, or were men more pugnacious in those days? We have improved in some things — is it the police or education?

John Mason, 1897

In some villages the older forms of amusement were of a very rough kind. There was a traditional fight that took place on Whit-Monday, between the Kaffirs — no doubt quite a recent corruption of Cavaliers — of Coneyhurst Hill in the Parish of Ewhurst, and the Diamond-topped Roundheads of Rudgwick, a village just over the Sussex border. It always took place at the 'Donkey' Inn at Cranleigh.

In former times there, were no doubt, many such fights in different parishes; they served to let off the superfluous youthful steam, that now finds an outlet in cricket and football.

Gertrude Jekyll, 1904

The working men of Guildford, mindful of the self respect that is expected of the working man in these progressive days turned a deaf ear to those who called for disturbances.

The *Surrey Adverstiser* 18th November 1864

What are we to make of the Guildford Guy Riots? These quotations provide the best explanations available from locals. They also fit in neatly with the views of other historians studying the social changes which took place in Victorian England. The boisterous Bonfire Night celebrations were a rural tradition suppressed by the authorities and abandoned by their supporters as society became more disciplined. R.D Storch has surveyed the 5th November celebrations in a number of Victorian towns. From his work it would appear that bonfire gangs like the Guildford Guys were a southern phenomenon which developed in Sussex, Surrey and Devon after the Napoleonic Wars and in Essex in the 1850s. The problem occurred in different towns at different times. Riots were taking place in Lewes in the 1840s and by the 1850s the authorities were trying to control the proceedings by recognising them officially. In 1853 the first two bonfire societies were formed and by 1863 the Brighton trains were taking excursionists to see the celebrations. At the other extreme the Chelmsford gentry and militia did not withdraw their patronage until 1860 and the riots and demonstrations which took place in the following years were not brought under control until 1888.

As the case of Guildford suggests the Bonfire Night demonstrations were not political movements. The supporters saw themselves as patriotic protestants maintaining popular rights and defying authority where necessary. The only national issue to be expressed was the 'Papal Aggression' in 1850. Local issues or complaints found expression in the festivities and this was, no doubt, why many respectable citizens feared them. In Guildford the issues expressed were no more than personal vendettas but in Oxford and Devon food-price riots in 1867 proceeded directly from the manifestations of the Fifth.

The troubles on Bonfire Night were ended in different ways. In Lewes, as we have seen, the authorities formally recognised the traditional Bonfire Night and today one can still see the sort of celebrations that were once common in Guildford. In Chelmsford the authorities brought an end to the popular celebrations by arranging their own properly organised festivities. In 1888 a bill published on the Fifth announced that there would be a torchlit procession, monster bonfire and town carnival on the Ninth. The Mayor and Corporation led the procession and by the 1890s the celebrations on the Fifth had been replaced by those on the Ninth.

In Guildford the activities of the Guys were totally suppressed. In 1866 there was calm in Guildford although a party of Guys did turn up in Godalming. The following year full precautions were taken and knots of men gathered on the street corners but only a few squibs were thrown about by boys and a few bonfires were lit on the outskirts of town. By 1870 the press noted 'scarcely a squib' in Guildford. Meanwhile official firework displays were organised to satisfy the desire of the inhabitants for some form of celebration. In 1867 and in succeeding years there were grand displays incorporating set pieces such as 'The destruction of Pompeii'. Bonfire night had started to take on its modern form in Guildford. One has to ask why the traditional festivities in Guildford were suppressed and not recognised or reformed as elsewhere? Without studying the peculiar circumstances in other towns it is difficult to answer this question. Possibly the failure of the Guildford authorities to take action allowed the problem to become so great that suppression was the only solution available or that opponents would tolerate. The involvement of the Home Office no doubt made reform near impossible.

Certain themes seem to run through the story of the Guys. We notice that central government was interfering in local affairs. Both the Bonfire Night celebrations and the chestnut fight at St Catherine's fell victim to tighter control from Westminster. Through direct interference and new legislation local independence was being reduced and policy was being decided in London. At the same time the authority of Guildford Town Council was increased as it was forced to take on more and more responsibilities. Society was becoming regulated more tightly whether it be at a local or national level. We often think of the Victorian reforms as progress. One cannot deny that they were improvements but the

Guy Riots remind us of what was lost. For better or for worse local traditions and, one could argue, some personal freedoms were suppressed as society came to expect more disciplined behaviour from all its members. This book is concerned with an isolated incident which produces only a limited amount of evidence. One has to be careful when make comments such as these.

Nevertheless it is worth reflecting on what we can learn. Having reached the end of the story of the Guys it is tempting to take a last look at the town and see how much it had changed since Henry Peak first arrived. Henry Peak's career seemed to follow the development of the town. A couple of years after their marriage the Peaks moved back to Commercial Road opposite Henry's old lodgings. There was room for an office but he was later able to afford an office in a separate house in Market Street. In 1862 Peak started laying out Guildford's first major estate — Charlotteville — on arable land bought by a local doctor, Thomas Sells. Two years later the Corporation acquired further powers under local government acts to take over the work of the Commission for Paving Lighting and Drainage. Peak answered an advert for the town's first borough surveyor and was appointed. Jacob was Mayor and opposed the appointment. Peak remembered him as a 'frank, outspoken gentlemen' but Jacob did at least accept the decision and visted Peak shortly afterwards. Although Jacob had opposed the appointment he said he had concluded that Peak was the right man and congratulated him on the way he had already taken up his duties. The post was not lucrative but it enabled Peak to make his mark on the town. Both the Castle Grounds and the famous setts in the High Street were among his many works.

Proper attempts to solve many of the inadequate services in the town seem to have coincided with Jacob's period in office. It would be interesting to look further into this man's impact on the town. By September 1863 the waterworks were in a very bad way. In recent years all the profits had been spent on laying new pipes to cope with the increased demand for water in the town. The water wheel was no longer able to meet the demand for the growing town and stopped altogether when the crank broke. Half the town's water came from springs and the remainder was pumped from the river. It was too dirty to even wash floorboards and one gentleman had discovered a fresh water shrimp in his water. The loss of the water wheel necessitated the construction of a steam pump. The water company, however, had lost its enthusiasm and decided to sell its shares to the town. Following a poll of the ratepayers in October the town took over the provision of water in 1866.

The fire service was still totally inadequate in 1863. In June a fire broke out a Mr Wilkin's Paper Mill in Stoke. It took the fire engine a hour and a half to reach the scene after the fire had been reported and for some reason there were no horses available so it had to be dragged by three or four men. Not surprisingly the mill was completely destroyed. The *West Surrey Times* on 15th August complained: 'We have three antiquated fire engines in the town whose latest improvement must be at least fifty years old. Our largest engine was the barrack engine, which was condemned forty-five years ago as unfit for use and beyond repair. It was, however, purchased by the Corporation and repaired. With regard to the two others, it is a question of whether the oldest inhabitant can tell their origin or the date of their manufacture. They run on wooden wheels and let out twice as much water as they throw'. Help came, however, for later in 1863 a volunteer fire brigade was set up and a horse-drawn fire engine purchased. By 1866 a second engine had be purchased by voluntary subscription. A shed was built in North Street and replaced by a proper brick fire station in 1872 designed by Henry Peak. The improvements in services stretched to medical provision. Building started on the Royal Surrey County Hospital in the Farnham Road in 1863 and it was opened in 1866.

＊   ＊   ＊   ＊

One leaves the story of the Guy Riots with a feeling that modern Guildford was starting to take shape. It was of course still very different from the town we know but attitudes and institutions that are very much part of modern Guildford were much more evident in 1866 than in 1851. One also has the feeling that there is so much more to discover. This story is about an isolated incident and there is undoubtedly a fair amount of distortion in the picture it presents. We only get a glimpse at the town but it is an intriguing glimpse and those who wish to look further into the history of Guildford will find plenty to reward their efforts.

BIBLIOGRAPHY

Most of the sources are identifiable from the text and I have tried to fill in the gaps below. The main sources of information are:

SURREY LOCAL STUDIES LIBRARY, GUILDFORD LIBRARY

PEAK, H., (manuscript), *Recollections and Activities as Mayor of Guildford, Volume D.*

MASON, J.,1897, *Guildford.*

GREEN, J.K.,1952, 'Fireworks, bonfires, illuminations and the Guy Riots' and 'Peace Officers in Guildford from 1367-1836', reprinted by permission of the *Surrey Times* in *Sidelights on Guildford History*

KEEP, *The Keep, the quarterly magazine of the Guildford Institute,* October 1912 and January 1913 — includes personal reminiscences of the Guys including the anonymous account in Chapter 1, Superintendent Law's account and the diary of a Surrey Volunteer as a special constable.

MORGAN, G., *Riot Control in Guildford during the Guy Riots (1842-1865),* (typewritten manuscript).

GUILDFORD, 1845, *A Descriptive and Historical View of the County Town of Surrey* — This was used for the account of the workhouse. The various guide books to Guildford and the directories are an invaluable source of information.

GUILDFORD MUNIMENT ROOM

BOROUGH OF GUILDFORD, *Minutes of the Meetings of the Watch Committee.* — Very useful for information about the police force.

THE BRITISH LIBRARY, NEWSPAPER LIBRARY, COLINDALE.

Sussex Advertiser and the Surrey Gazette
West Surrey Times
Surrey Advertiser (also on microfilm in the Surrey Local Studies Library.)
The Times

PUBLIC RECORDS OFFICE, KEW

All the correspondence between Guildford and the Home Office is to be found here under reference numbers: HO45 7324; HO45 7443; HO45 7442; HO45 8369; HO45 40850; HO45 5128N.

UNIVERSITY OF LONDON, SENATE HOUSE

Acts of Parliament and summaries of the census returns (although the information on Wood Street comes from SMITH, N (ed.) *Wood Street*).

OTHER SOURCES

ALEXANDER, M., (1986, reprinted 1992 by Ammonite Books, Godalming), *Guildford—A Short History* — The most up to date general history.

CHAMBERLAIN, E.R., *Guildford—A Biography.*

GOLBY, J.M. AND PURDUE, A.W., (1984), *The Civilisation of the Crowd-Popular Culture in England 1750-1900.*

JEKYLL, G., (1904, reprinted 1978 by Kohler and Combes, Dorking), *Old West Surrey.* A wonderful description of rural life in the last century.

MORGAN, G., (1985), 'The Guildford Guy Riots (1842-1865)' in *Surrey Archaeological Collections* Vol 76.

RICHTER, D.C., (1981) *Riotous Victorians*

SMITH, N. (ed.), (1988), *Wood Street—The Growth of a Village.*

STORCH, R.D. 'Please to Remember the Fifth of November: Conflict, Solidarity and Public Order in Southern England, 1815–1900' in Storch (ed.) *Popular Culture and Custom in 19th Century England.*

GENERAL NOTES ON CHAPTERS

ILLUSTRATIONS

The map at the front of the book comes from Guildford Museum. All the line drawings except where specified below come from Victorian guides and directories to Guildford in the Surrey Local Studies Library.

CHAPTER I — LONDON: 1605

There is a good account of the Gunpowder Plot in the *Dictionary of National Biography*. ILLUSTRATIONS: Guy Fawkes laying the fuse by George Cruikshank (Museum of London).

CHAPTER II — HENRY PEAK MEETS THE GUYS

For information on riots in other towns I have used STORCH. GREEN provides the background to Bonfire Night in Guildford prior to the Guy Riots. ILLUSTRATIONS: Guy Fawkes celebrations from Pyne's *Costumes of Great Britain*, 1808 (Museum of London).

CHAPTER III — GUILDFORD IN 1851

Where no source is indicated in the text it can be assumed that the information comes from *The Sussex Advertiser* and *The Surrey Gazette* for 1851. The information on the workhouse comes from *Guildford-A Descriptive . . . View* (1845). The guides, almanacs and directories in the Surrey Local Studies Library were also used for basic facts on other institutions and public services. ILLUSTRATIONS: Guildford Union Workhouse (Guildford Museum). Family enjoying Bonfire Night from the *Illustrated London News* November 1849 (Museum of London).

CHAPTER IV — SOMETHING MUST BE DONE!

See GREEN for background to the Guildford Police and also the *Minutes of the Watch Committee* in the Muniment Room. The information for this chapter has been taken from a variety of sources which are recorded in detail in MORGAN, G., *Riot Control in Guildford*. ILLUSTRATIONS: Metropolitan Policemen during the Chartist Excitement from the *Illustrated London News* 12th June 1848 (Museum of London).

CHAPTER V — BATTLE COMMENCES

ILLUSTRATIONS: Policemen fighting crowds: 1. Reform Rights 1832 from Metropolitan Police Historical Museum. 2. Troops departing at Euston from the *Illustrated London News* August 1842.

CHAPTER VI — GUILDFORD IN 1858

Most of the information for this chapter comes from *The West Surrey Times* for 1858. ILLUSTRATIONS: An Election Scene (Guildford Museum).

CHAPTER VIII — A TOWN IN DISGRACE

The accounts of the Royal Wedding celebrations and St Catherine's Fair come from the *West Surrey Times* (14th March 1863 and 10th October 1863). ILLUSTRATIONS: St Catherine's Fair after J.M.W. Turner, 1832.

CHAPTER IX — THE END

The preparations leading up to the 5th November are from the correspondence with the Home Office. Otherwise the information comes from the newspapers mentioned in the text. See the *West Surrey Times* 7th November to 19th December. For Superintendent Law's account and the diary of the Surrey Volunteer who acted as special constable see *The Keep*. Jacob's account is published in the *Surrey Advertiser* for 21st March 1868. The debate over raising the pay of the police comes form the *Surrey Advertiser* for 11th November 1865 and the final riots are recorded in the same paper for 20th December 1865 and 6th January 1866 and the trial is in the April edition. ILLUSTRATIONS: Photographs of Guildford Policemen (Surrey Local Studies Library). Policeman facing rioters from *Punch* 11th August 1866 (Museum of London).

CHAPTER X — EPILOGUE

STORCH is the source for information on 5th November in other towns. The details of Guildford at the end of the riots come from the newspapers and Peak's Diary Volume D. References to the water supply can be found in the *West Surrey Times* for 22nd August 1863, 12th September 1863, 26th September 1863, 3rd October 1863. The references to the fire service come from the same newspaper for 27th June 1863 and 15th August 1863.